YOUR ONLY CHILD

Your
Only Child

—

ANNE COATES

BLOOMSBURY

For my daughter Olivia

Acknowledgements

I would like to thank all the people who gave up their time to share their thoughts and experiences. All names have been changed to protect privacy. My heartfelt thanks are also due to friends who supported me in the writing of this book by entertaining my daughter while I was working.

First published 1996 by Bloomsbury publishing Plc, 2 Soho Square, London W1V 6HB
Copyright © 1996 by Anne Coates
The moral right of the author has been asserted
A copy of the CIP entry for this book is available from the British Library

ISBN 0 7475 2164 6

10 9 8 7 6 5 4 3 2 1

Designed by Hugh Adams, AB3

Typeset by Hewer Text Composition Services, Edinburgh

Printed in Great Britain by
Cox & Wyman Ltd, Reading, Berkshire

Contents

Preface

I HAVE a vested interest in writing this book: I'm the mother of a single child, my seven-year-old daughter Olivia. From Olivia's second birthday onwards people have been asking me when I'm going to produce a sibling for her (I have no intention of doing so!) and then giving me the benefit of their wisdom about the only child and the likelihood that they will become spoilt, lonely and insufferable. My daughter is none of these. She is a joy to me just as children in larger families are to their parents. However, the many parents of only children I have talked to and I work hard to make sure our children don't miss out by not having siblings, and that they live fulfilled and happy lives. Parenting is a difficult job however many children you have, and if you have just one child you only get one chance to get it right.

You also have no benchmark within the immediate family to judge behaviour by – although this is often a blessing! So it's useful to talk to other parents both of only children and of siblings to put your own child's behaviour in context. In this book lots of parents of only children discuss their experiences in various situations. I have also included the views of adult onlies on their childhoods and how being an only has affected them in later life. I have tried to cover all aspects of bringing up a single child in a variety of family configurations, and have set out practical guides for things like encouraging your child to make friends, or joining a step-family where there are more children.

Writing this book has confirmed for me that only children do not suffer as a result of not having brothers and sisters and

I sincerely hope it will help bury some of the myths about only children and act as a guide for those who have also decided or are contemplating limiting their families to one offspring.

Anne Coates, 1996.

Introduction

Chapter 1
One-child families: the reasons

ARE ONE-CHILD FAMILIES NEW?

Why do some couples produce only one offspring? Is there something in their own make-up? Are some people automatically more likely to limit their family size than others? Whatever the reasons, one thing is clear: families with only children have never been regarded as ideal.

Historically there were sound reasons for having a large family, the prime one being that up to almost the middle of this century many babies did not survive the first two years and lots of children died from diseases that are today non-existent or curable. A large family made sense economically: there were more hands to work in the fields or factories. And when the parents grew old there was always someone around to look after them.

We have moved away from that kind of society. Families have shrunk and geographical mobility means that most of us no longer live with or even near our extended families. One direct result of this is that parents have less help with childcare from their families and therefore may be more likely to limit their family size. Gone are the days when Granny or Auntie lived round the corner and was always on call for a spot of babysitting: these days even if grandmothers live nearby they are quite likely to have jobs or commitments of their own, making them unavailable.

Our society has changed dramatically since the Second World War, with far more women continuing to work after marriage, but our attitudes to families and what they should be like have not. There's still a very strong social obligation to provide a sibling for a first-born child, regardless of the family's circumstances.

In particular, despite these changes in our society and the ways in which we bring up children, there are still some people who think that sibling relationships are the only ones which provide the correct experiences for proper social development. The theory is that if a child doesn't have brothers and sisters she can't possibly be a normal, healthy, well-brought-up individual, and there's bound to be something wrong with her – she's lonely, maladjusted and selfish! Throughout this look I show that it's the quality of parenting that matters, and that many assumptions about the value of families with many children are simply wrong.

Some of our society's assumptions:

- A second child won't cost you any more – you've already made all the major purchases. But children cost more as they get older and you can never guarantee that one child will fit into her older sibling's clothes and shoes! If you have children of different sexes clothes can't necessarily be passed on and you will have to provide an extra bedroom when they get older.
- Only children get a bad press: whenever they commit a crime, it's mentioned as though it's a contributing factor. The Hungerford gunman, Michael Ryan, received, according to neighbours, 'the usual over-attention of a single child'.
- All misbehaviour is because the child is an only and thus by definition is spoilt and badly behaved when she doesn't get her own way.
- The parents of single children are themselves selfish.

As I explore in part two, 'Family Issues', today's families come in all shapes and sizes from huge extended families all living together to single parents and couples of the same sex bringing up children together; and however hard the 'ideal' of a nuclear family is still promoted, with two parents and two children, preferably one of each sex, it is becoming much less the norm.

4

Table 1: Family composition in Great Britain

	1972	1975	1981	1991
Couples + one child	16	17	18	17
Couples + two or more	76	74	70	66
Lone mother + one child	2	3	3	5
Lone mother + two or more	5	6	7	12
Lone father + one child	-	-	1	-
Lone father + two or more	1	1	1	1
Sample size	9474	9293	8216	5799

(From *Social Trends 23*, 1993 edition, 'Percentages of families with one child in GB')

There are and always have been women and families who have just one child, and for a variety of historical and social and personal reasons. In the 1920s, after the First World War, one in five women had an only child. By the 1950s this had dropped to 13 per cent and, as you can see from Table 2 was expected to remain consistent, although it now seems that only children have been on the increase, as Table 1 showed.

Table 2: The projected number of children per woman in England and Wales (based on women's expectations)

Year of birth of woman	Average number of children per woman	Number of children (percentages)				
		0	1	2	3	4 or more
1950	2.06	14	13	42	20	10
1955	1.99	17	13	40	19	10
1960	1.95	19	13	40	18	10
1965	1.97	17	13	41	19	10
1970	2.02	16	12	42	19	11
1975	2.02	17	13	41	19	9

(OPCS, *Population projections 1987–2027*, Series PP2 no.16, 'Mid-1987-based projections of numbers of children per woman, England and Wales')

However, the reasons for women and families having one child in the past – due to wars, the Depression and so on – are not necessarily applicable to current one-child families. The relative increase in the number of only children in recent years may be due to any one or a combination of factors that are particular to the age we live in:

- improvements in contraception and its availability
- more women taking up careers
- economic factors – high housing costs, an unstable job market
- more marriages breaking up
- women deciding to have a baby on their own and stopping at one

While having two or three children is still seen as the 'norm' by the majority of people in Britain, in Hungary one in four families has an only child. The number of single-child families is also high in Italy (surprisingly as this is a Catholic country!), Germany and the USA and, of course, China has imposed a policy of limiting families to one child. In fact much of the research on only children has been carried out in studies in China. However their culture is very different to ours, and you cannot compare the way adults bring up a child who has no siblings (probably against their own wishes) because of a state law with parents who have voluntarily limited their family.

WILL YOUR ONLY CHILD SUFFER?

The parents of only children I have talked to saw as a main advantage the fact that they didn't have to divide their time and their child didn't have to compete with siblings for parental attention. This was especially true if both parents worked. Many parents, aware of the sibling rivalry in their own families when they were children (and who are perhaps still coming to terms with it – the classic film *Whatever Happened to Baby Jane*, starring Bette Davis and Joan Crawford, says it all!) are happy for their offspring to avoid it. Parents with limited financial resources also feel that they can better provide for one child without having to make too many compromises or sacrifices. And certainly only children enjoy much more personal privacy and less disruption in their lives.

Advantages	Disadvantages
● avoid sibling rivalry	● miss sibling companionship
● more parental attention	● more pressure to succeed
● enjoy greater affluence	● too much adult company
● more privacy	● unwelcome solitude

The disadvantages of missing out on sibling company can be overcome by following certain strategies which will be elaborated upon in Part One – 'The Child'.

The advantages and disadvantages of being an only child can be expressed in terms of personality. However, these are very general statements, and as later chapters show, the personality of any child is dependant on a great many factors, not least the personalities of her parents!

Advantages	Disadvantages
● self-contained	● expects people to anticipate her needs
● self-sufficient	● secretive
● conscientious	● impatient with others
● outspoken in likes and dislikes	● touchy if left out
● loyal and faithful	● a poor competitor and inexperienced loser

I feel there are so many positive facets to being an only child that the advantages far outweigh any perceived disadvantages, which can all be compensated for, as I will show.

As a friend of mine said as she tried to juggle the demands of her toddler and baby as well as her six-and-a-half-year-old son, 'They say there are compensatory factors in having more than one child but I can't see any. All I feel is guilty that I can't do all the things I used to do with Jamie. I feel he's the one who's missing out most. He now has so little of my time and attention.

Who are the women who have just one child?

I spoke to a number of women to find out whether it was a conscious choice on their part or whether circumstances beyond their control made the decision for them. Career, age of parents, financial considerations, breakdown of a relationship and health as well as a personal preference for having a single child were some of the reasons they gave. Most of the ones I spoke to had no regrets and those that did found there were compensations.

Career women

Nowadays women who wish to establish themselves in a career often make a conscious decision to leave their child-bearing until they are in their thirties. Unlike men, who don't have to take a career break or at least a few months off work when they start a family, women have to plan their pregnancies very carefully. By the time they have completed their training and started to establish themselves in a career many women find that although they have spent years actively trying to avoid pregnancy, when they want to conceive their fertility is in question.

Other women who plan to have careers have one child early, perhaps thinking they'll have another at some unspecified time in the future. Both the older and younger mothers discover that by having just one child a career is less disrupted, and it's also easier to combine the demands of their work and their relationship with parenthood when they only have one child to consider.

Hilary was quite adamant that she only ever wanted one child and that one child was compatible with her demanding job as head of design in a college.

> *Maybe because I am an only child I only ever wanted one child. I found the whole process of giving birth gruesome and I felt awful for a long time afterwards. I couldn't envisage going through that again. It took a long time to get back into gear both physically and mentally. I went back to work after eight weeks. There are cycles in education and fortunately I had my baby in the autumn term which isn't quite so frantic as the*

8

others. I consider my job physically and mentally exhausting. It would definitely take too much planning to have another child and childcare costs would be considerably more. In fact I did get pregnant again and was prepared to have a termination but I miscarried.

For other career women the 'right' moment to have a second child never seems to arrive. Yvonne, an account manager in a bank, was twenty-three when she had Dorian, now aged sixteen.

I thought perhaps I'd have another one later but I wanted to continue my career. I was very career-orientated and I did have complications with Dorian's birth. I think I would have liked to have about three children and sometimes I regret that but I don't think I'd be doing the job I have now if I'd had more. I'm looking forward to being a granny!

Another consideration for the working mother is that childcare becomes increasingly complicated and more expensive with each addition to the family; often siblings are in different locations, so that delivering and collecting have to be planned with military precision and woe betide you if you suddenly have to work late.

Money matters

Economics and financial considerations play a progressively important role in deciding family size as Jenny, a solicitor, is only too aware.

I earn more than my husband Tony and my salary pays the mortgage. Tony was keener than I to have a baby but once pregnant, I loved the baby. When Luke was born I loved having a baby and didn't want to go back to work. While I was pregnant we sold one house and bought another and the profit we made paid for me to have six months off work as I would only have had the statutory maternity leave and pay.

When Luke was two I persuaded Tony we could take out a second mortgage to cover my maternity leave for a second baby. Unfortunately a survey revealed our house had subsidence and a remortgage was out of the question. I'd have had another baby and gone back to work after three months but Tony says that wouldn't be fair to the baby. Luke is now six and a half and the biological urge is fading. I would have loved another but I have to live with the fact that that is out of the question. And I have to admit that I do enjoy being able to devote myself to my son. The other day it was my birthday and we went out to lunch together. It was really lovely and we sat and talked about all sorts of things. I know that if I'd had more children the meal out would probably have been too expensive for us and that other children would have changed the dynamics anyway.

Single parent – divorced

Some parental relationships break up before a second child is conceived, and with no new partner on the horizon the first child is destined to be an only, perhaps by default, as Fran revealed.

I never saw myself as a single parent or the mother of an only child, but now I'm both. My marriage broke up about six weeks after my daughter was born and due to this I also had to go back to work much sooner than I'd planned. Before I had my baby I felt strongly that I would need the support of a partner and I would never have contemplated having a child on my own. Now I realize I don't need a man around.

In an ideal world I would have liked to have more than one child but I am not keen on having different fathers for my children. For Marnie's sake I encourage strong links with my sister's family, who live in the same road as us. It's the main reason we moved here. She also went to nursery when I went back to work so she's always had lots of other children around during the day.

My relationship with my sister has always been good – I see a sister as someone who's always there for you, although I know other people haven't enjoyed that sort of relationship with their siblings. I feel that being mixed race, having a sister or a brother to share things she may not be able to share with me would be an advantage for Marnie. But as that isn't to be we have to work at it in different ways. There are a lot of mixed-race families in the area and we became friendly with some while still at nursery so we can compare experiences and support each other.

For me as a single parent, I wouldn't consider having another child as I simply couldn't afford it. At the moment we do quite nicely. I have a good job and my finances don't have to be stretched too far. Before I had Marnie I had always considered adoption as a possibility for me but now I feel it wouldn't be right for us. It could jeopardize everything.

Single parent – no relationship

Some women who have never given much thought to motherhood suddenly find that the biological urge to reproduce gets stronger in their thirties. If you aren't married or living in a stable relationship but have your own home and a reasonable income single-parenthood can seem an acceptable alternative, as Kathy discovered.

My relationship broke up because of my pregnancy. I don't think it was a conscious decision to get pregnant but I certainly wasn't unhappy to discover I was going to have a baby. The man I was with gave me an ultimatum: have an abortion or lose me. I think he was rather stunned that I refused a termination. I was in my mid-thirties and I realized this was probably my one and only chance to be a mother and I grabbed it with both hands.

I had a very easy pregnancy and when my daughter was born I was overwhelmed by my feelings for her. Nothing could have prepared me for the love I felt. In fact no man could compete! Although I enjoyed being pregnant and had a wonderful delivery, I didn't really consider having another child. I certainly adored having a baby to look after and care for and as she got older I did miss that side of it (I suppose that's why some women keep on having babies) but I knew I didn't have the energy and resources for more children.

I don't think my daughter misses out because she doesn't have a brother or a sister – in fact I think she positively benefits from being on her own. She has plenty of friends and she also sees a lot of her cousins and the rest of the family. Of course she doesn't see her father or his family but then nor do lots of children whose parents divorce. On the whole I think we're both very happy with our situation.

Only-child mother

For some women there has never been any question of having more than one child. Marian is one such woman. She is an only child herself and made a positive decision to repeat her own family pattern.

I can't say I had a wonderfully happy childhood but being an only had nothing to do with that. I don't get on with my mother – as far as I'm concerned she's a total cow. For that reason we've had long periods when we've lost contact with each other. However I had a fantastic relationship with my dad and we were really close. We were very poor but I didn't want for anything because there was only one child. That was one of the reasons my parents didn't have any more. The other was that my mother refused to go through with the whole awful process again – as she never ceased telling me.

I made a very conscious decision to limit my family to one child. I need some time for me. I enjoy my work and intended carrying on after my daughter was born. I don't think one child suffers when a mother goes back to work as they haven't got to share her time. However I would have felt obliged to give up work if I'd had more children and I don't think I'd then have been a good mother. My husband is the youngest of thirteen and originally he wanted more than one. I said, 'Let's have one and see how it goes.' Since then he's been happy to stick with one. He's a bit of a workaholic and maybe he thought he'd have to help more if we had more children, I don't know. We both wanted a girl and had one so in a way there was never the temptation to have another.

I was never lonely as a child and nor has my daughter been. Since she was seven months she's been child-minded two days a week with older and younger kids. She went to toddler club and all the usual things before school and she makes friends so easily that she's only on her own when she wants to be. She would love a brother, so – in a way – we've adopted one. My friend's son is three-and-a-half and both families do lots of things together.

We also do lots of things with Lauren on our own. When we go out to dinner she comes too and on holiday she's included in more grown-up activities as well as the usual children's ones. She gets to experience an awful lot. I think most people underestimate children and don't give them credit for enjoying things other than Disney and TV.

Medical and physical reasons

Many women are now delaying having their children and this may be one reason why single-child families are on the increase. By her mid-thirties a woman's fertility starts to decline more rapidly, making it more difficult to conceive or sustain a pregnancy – as Julie discovered.

When Fanny was three-and-a-half I had very mixed views about only children – they could turn into spoilt brats if you're not careful – but there again I know a lot of adults who are only children and they are quite balanced and easy-going.

Fanny might end up being an only child. At first I didn't try for another due to financial reasons. Then when we decided we could afford to have another, I had two miscarriages. Probably due to these I feel I really want another baby and I'm still hoping to have one but as Fanny is now six she will have spent her formative years as an only child anyway. I work full time and I can see it is a lot more stressful having two children. My mother says it's better to look after one properly rather than two less well and as long as I've got one I should be happy (and she has four). I'm still trying for a baby but feel that at thirty-nine age is definitely against me.'

Other women have a health condition which may prevent them having more than one child. Geraldine has multiple sclerosis, a condition which gets progressively worse with any setback.

I was delighted to find myself pregnant. It wasn't planned. I was monitored very closely while I was pregnant. However I did manage to have a totally natural delivery. It was fabulous. But afterwards my speech went for a week. I was terrified it wouldn't come back. I've coped well with Natalie, who's now six. But I don't like asking people for help so I really wouldn't contemplate having another baby.

The baby with special needs

Sometimes the only child is born with some form of handicap or disability. Many parents believe it is better to devote themselves to the care of a special needs baby rather than risk having another. Maggie was one such woman.

My daughter was born with cystic fibrosis. Looking after her took all my energy and I wouldn't have contemplated having another baby with the risk that entailed. My marriage broke up partly due to the strain of looking after my daughter. Initially her prognosis wasn't good but she has survived well into her twenties and in fact has a son of her own now. With all her health problems, I thought she was mad to have a baby but she has lived independently from me for some time.

PARENTAL FEARS
Missing out on siblings

There's no guarantee that having a brother or sister will improve a child's life in any way. Many siblings simply do not get on with each other and are constantly bickering and vying for their parents' attention. My own daughter often comments on this after she's been to visit friends with siblings and responds positively to being an only.

We can't play with him as much and we feel guilty

Adults can never be a substitute for having other children to play with. Many parents of onlies actively encourage having friends to play, arranging sleepovers etc (see Chapters Four and Five) so that their child doesn't miss out on playing with peers and they don't always have to engage in children's activities themselves!

Loneliness

Only children don't seem to suffer from loneliness any more than children with siblings. Even children from large families can find themselves playground wallflowers and strategies have to be found to overcome this (see Chapters Four and Five for some solutions and practical advice). Obviously loneliness can especially affect only children when there is a crisis in the family, such as a death or divorce, but this usually means that the parent or adult who is caring for that child hasn't handled the situation very well. See Chapter Twelve for detailed advice on coping with bereavement.

When we've gone she'll be on her own

Many parents feel that with siblings their children will have someone else to be with after their death, but although some brothers and sisters maintain a strong family commitment many do not, and you can never be certain which category your family will fit into. The most important thing for any child is to learn to establish and work at friendships, and to build a network of support systems to help her throughout life.

As we grow older and more infirm she'll have to shoulder all the responsibility on her own

In an ideal world people would plan for their old age. Just as we take out pensions so too we should think about what we would like to happen to us in different sets of circumstances. For instance, we might prefer to go into a home for the elderly if we become infirm and not invade a child's home with demands that she might not be able to meet. However the world is not an ideal place and the people in it are far from perfect. It is usually one child who shoulders the burden of ageing parents while others in the family avoid the issue. This can lead to much heartache and resentment within a family and rifts that are never healed.

Summary

Parents have one child for many reasons from a firm commitment to the idea of having an only, to fate taking a hand and dictating that no other child will follow. People's background, age, financial status, health, career prospects and whether or not they are in a relationship and what that relationship is like all have a bearing on family size.

Chapter 2
Exploding the myths

'Only children are spoiled, lonely and maladjusted.'

spoil   *injure the child's character by excessive indulgence*
lonely   *solitary, companionless, isolated*
maladjusted   *unable to adapt or cope with the demands of a social environment*
(from the Concise Oxford Dictionary*)*

Children are born egotists – they all think that the world revolves around them and their needs. A baby sees her mother only in terms of what she provides; she is there to nourish, nurture and cherish and she has no other role in life. Young children are convinced that their parents have no other existence, no needs of their own to be satisfied or taken into consideration and still see the parent as extensions of themselves – and on call night and day! Part of the growing-up process involves coming to terms with the fact that this is not so. I expect we all know a few adults who have not learned this essential fact of life. However the chances are that these immature adults are not necessarily only children. Egotism and immaturity are not the particular preserves of the only child.

To explode the myths, we have to define what only children are. From a developmental point of view, siblings, including half- and step-siblings who are six or more years older are effectively onlies. A child who is younger by even four years is hardly a playmate for her older sibling: they will be at different stages of development and won't enjoy the same games or toys. They may, of course, master the skill of sharing their parents' time and attention and learn to be kind and supportive to each other and respect the other's privacy and rights but one look at many families with more than one child reveals an amazing amount of rivalry and competition, sometimes expressed in physical violence and bad behaviour, that often remains unresolved and lingers into adulthood.

All first-born children are onlies until number two arrives and a proportion of these will remain onlies for some time, holding centre-stage with no one else to share the limelight. First-borns and onlies obviously have similar experiences but it is interesting to note that research has shown that mothers who have made a firm decision to have one child react differently to their offspring than mothers who expect to have more children.

Popular myths about only children

Although research shows that only children are no more likely to be spoiled, lonely or maladjusted than children with siblings (see Chapter Three), the stereotypical idea of the single child in a family persists and mostly people's ideas about an only child are based on rather suspect or subjective views that can't be substantiated. An example is the idea that only children must be spoilt. When many people use the word they are not implying the dictionary definition, but rather that the child receives a lot of love, attention, toys, outings or whatever. They usually mean indulged, and that is rather different. This is true in Bob's case, describing his family:

> I was a widower and brought up my four boys on my own. It was hard organizing all the babysitting and childcare while I worked full-time but I was determined to keep the family together. When my boys were all grown up I met Sharon and we have one son, Liam, who is now eight. Liam's life is completely different. He's really spoilt. For a start he has his mother to look after him as well but he also has four older brothers who adore him. At Christmas he get four trips to Hamleys! I think he leads a charmed life but he's a smashing little lad and he's got loads of friends at school and is doing really well.

While four trips to Hamleys may seem excessive, Bob doesn't really mean that he is bringing up a little boy who is selfish, or uncaring. In comparison to his older sons' early life, Liam's life is very different – for a start he hasn't lost his mother. But it hardly seems that all the extra attention of four indulgent older brothers is turning his head.

The problem is that findings from modern research have not permeated through into the popular consciousness. People still have misguided ideas about only children and this is reinforced by the media perpetuating the idea. The myth is even unquestioned by some onlies including one actor I spoke to who was emphatic that every only child was spoilt – because he had been.

> *I was an only myself and I think I was spoilt. My mother didn't have much money so she bought me a second-hand bike. I wanted a new one and created such a fuss my mother went round all the relatives and managed to collect enough money to buy me a new one.*

How sad that this man should condemn his mother so roundly and not appreciate her predicament, her desire to give him what he really wanted. It's an uphill struggle to convince this man and those like him that not all only children are spoilt. One mother told me how furious she felt when she took her child to visit a particular school friend for the first time:

> *The child's mother, who had five children aged from five to eighteen, immediately told me I should supply my daughter with a baby brother or sister as only children were lonely and spoilt. My daughter had just spent a wonderful summer enjoying all sorts of activities with a wide variety of friends and family while this woman's children had been more or less confined to the home as they had each other to play – and fight! – with.*
>
> *At the end of our visit the mother congratulated me on how I was bringing up my daughter, complimenting me on her behaviour and manners, etc. I realize she probably didn't mean to but she sounded so patronizing and condescending –*

*as if she had some sort of right to judge and comment on my
child-rearing skills.*

All children misbehave from time to time but the chances are, if
you have an only, other people will assume her misbehaviour
comes from not having a brother or sister. Even the parents of
only children themselves find they're inadvertently contributing
to the myth, as Joanne remembers.

*I must admit I feel quite sensitive about criticism levelled at me
for having an only child and I often find myself watching my
daughter's behaviour as though I'm waiting for her to turn out
delinquent! That's an exaggeration but you know what I mean, I
don't want her to be badly thought of. One time we went
swimming with a friend who has three children. Afterwards my
daughter asked for a packet of crisps 'from the machine' because
that was what we usually did. My friend however handed her one
of the packets she'd bought with her from home. This wasn't
good enough for Ashley and she threw a real wobbly almost
screaming at me to buy her a packet from the machine.*

*I must admit I didn't handle it very well. I felt really
embarrassed by the scene Ashley was causing, convinced that
everyone was thinking, 'There goes a spoilt only child.' My
friend insisted that it was far too expensive to buy all the kids
crisps from the machine and while I agreed with her on one
level I realized I had in fact let Ashley down. It looked as though
she was acting like a spoilt brat but in fact I'd reneged on our
deal which was that we always bought a little something to eat
after swimming and she was still too young at four to understand why this time was different. I felt really awful afterwards
because I'd let the larger family dictate what we did as though
they were allowed to by sheer strength of numbers.*

Academic myths and modern studies

Until comparatively recently psychiatrists and psychologists
tended to see only negative aspects in being an only child. Child
development expert D. W. Winnicott, in *The Child, the Family and
the Outside World* (Penguin, 1964) refers to the 'immense

disadvantages' of an only child and states that it is both important and valuable for a child to witness his mother as pregnant:

'. . . I think that every child who has missed such an experience, and who has never seen mother giving milk from her breasts, and bathing and caring for an infant, is less rich than the child who has witnessed these things.'

So much for the younger or youngest child in a family, who like an only is thus disadvantaged in not seeing her mother in this caring role! In one short sentence Winnicott has written them all off.

Fortunately psychologists have moved on quite considerably from this viewpoint and, as will be shown throughout this book, later and current research tends to disprove previously perceived disadvantages in being an only child.

One study (included in *Single Child Family*, ed. Toni Fablo, 1984) showed that mothers of three-month-old onlies were more socially interactive both with their infants and with others than mothers of first-borns. The mothers of onlies smiled and touched their babies more and by the time they reached twenty-four months mothers of onlies tended to show more approval of their child especially in relation to playing with toys. In this study onlies came into contact with a smaller number of people but more frequently than the first-borns.

Initially only babies initiated more interaction, and tended to smile and play less and cry more. However these differences had disappeared by the time the babies were twelve months old.

Much has been written about birth order and its significance for the individual – parenting magazines seem to produce an annual article on the subject – and there are a few general and generalized conclusions to be drawn. First-born children, it is said, tend to suffer from their parents' inexperience and anxiety but are more likely to be high achievers. In a home observation study carried out by Lewis and Kreitzber in 1979 (*Single Child Family* ed. Toni Fablo, 1984), it was found that children spaced more than four years apart were treated more like first-borns than later borns. Maybe this is because, as parents, we tend to forget very quickly what the early stages with a baby are like and so it is like starting again with a child who arrives some four years later. The second child benefits from more relaxed parenting and 'tutoring' from an older sibling, who is however often resented for the real or imagined privileges of age while at the same time adored for her achievements. If the second child is one of three she can lack attention, as the youngest is likely to be pampered and 'babied'.

The only child's experiences match some of those for the oldest and youngest children in a family. The age differences and sex of siblings also influence how parents relate to them and they to each other. Each child is unique and, of course all sorts of other factors like culture, environment and religion come into play. 'The overwhelming message of these studies', writes Ann Laybourn (*Children and Society* (volume 4, no. 4), 1990), 'is that only children, far from suffering as many parents fear, do well by any standards.'

PARENT TRAPS: YOU AND YOUR ONLY CHILD

Is she alone or lonely?

There is a world of difference between being alone and feeling lonely. You can feel lonely in a crowd of people – and many people do. Of the adult only children I spoke to, relatively few mentioned ever feeling lonely. Yet people still make amazing assumptions about how a single child in a family feels. Neighbours have said to me of my daughter, 'Oh, she must get lonely.' But why? Her life is full – her social commitments are far more interesting than mine! As many adults will testify, you can feel lonely in a family when you don't get on with your brother or sister and their friends. I certainly don't feel that loneliness is a condition of being a single child, but if you're worried about your child, read the Action Box *Is your child lonely?* in Chapter Four and then if you feel she is lonely follow the guidelines to improve her condition.

Is she maladjusted or well adjusted?

There is no evidence to suggest that only children behave any more unacceptably than children with brothers and sisters. Having a sibling doesn't necessarily prepare you for life in a wider social context. All that can really be said is that having a sibling teaches you to live alongside and with a sibling. It doesn't prepare you for marriage or working with colleagues as part of a team. How a child turns out is not dependent on the size of its family, but on the genes it was born with and the circumstances of that family and the environment it was brought up in. All children have to be taught social skills (see Chapter Five to find out how) and onlies are no less effective in social situations than anybody else.

Are you spoiling your child?

You cannot spoil a child with love but love is not the same thing as giving in to every whim and wish expressed by your offspring. You are spoiling your child if you:

- allow him always to dictate what you watch on television
- provide another type of meal when he has refused something that was previously his favourite (a way round this, as one mother found, was to consistently offer bread and butter as the alternative)
- always buy sweets, treats and toys on demand
- always let him have his own way

A spoiled child will:

- refuse to accept another's point of view
- give up on games he's not winning
- insist on his own way
- bully other children (and maybe his parents)
- refuse to cooperate at organized gatherings like a child's party or school sports day

'PARENTS OF ONLY CHILDREN ARE SELFISH'

This is another very popular myth whose origin may be explained by the fact that other parents are often envious of those with a sole child – and, let's face it, there are lots of advantages in terms of time and effort. One child is less disruptive to the lives of her parents, so those parents are branded as selfish; and they are also often seen as less committed to the idea of being a parent and more to being a fulfilled adult with adult interests. But however many children we have, most of us have to balance their demands with our own needs, and what, I wonder, is so awful about acknowledging we have needs? I often hear so-called committed mothers complaining about the lack of time for themselves and their own interests.

Women seem to be more harshly judged than their partners. Women who are 'giving in to their biological urges' are damned and then ignored by feminists: by their less ideologically concerned sisters who have more than one child, a woman producing only one is 'committed to her career or interests'. Basically, through other people's eyes, if you're the parent of an only you just can't win!

However, it might be that other parents are really rather envious of those with smaller families and try to justify their own position by denigrating others. Parents who are struggling financially to bring up two or three children may make barbed comments about the holidays or new clothes you're able to afford having just one child to cater for. Really, of course, the reasons for having only one are far more varied and complex.

One mother pointed out how she didn't see her decision to have one child as selfish in any way.

I don't think we're selfish having just one child. We enjoy Gerard enormously. We enjoy being with him and having him as part of our lives. Now that he's older (eight) he's a smashing, relaxed little companion. He's not competing for our attention. When I see some families where the parents are made distraught by all the demands being made on them, I think, 'Is it really worth the hassle?'

It seems to me a rather selfless act to limit your family to one in spite of the fact that you might want more out of consideration for that child, as another mother explained.

I don't think of myself as selfish. Rather the opposite, in fact. When I had my baby I knew she was going to be an only as I was in my mid-thirties and would be bringing her up on my own. I got to know a group of other first-time mothers and gradually, one by one, they all became pregnant again – the first one producing a second child after only fifteen months. Initially I felt rather envious as I loved babies and I had loved being pregnant. I suppose it would have been relatively easy to get pregnant again but that would have been a selfish act. I can afford one child and can give her a good home. Another child would have stretched my resources – and me – too far.

In some circumstances having more than one child can be a selfish act, as one mother of three boys told me, 'If I'd had a girl first time, I definitely wouldn't have had any more children. I love my sons but if I thought I could be sure of a girl next time I'd have another baby.'

Often being an only child oneself can make you more likely to want just one child yourself, as Anne said. 'I had a wonderful childhood. I never missed having a brother or sister and I don't see why my only son should.'

Another only was less enthusiastic about her own childhood but had no reservations about having an only herself.

I wouldn't say my childhood was ecstatic. My mother didn't really like or want children but in her way she was quite devoted to me. She continued working and I just got on with life, often going to their shop after school. I don't think I'm particularly maternal either but when I was in my thirties there was a definite urge to reproduce and I'm more than happy with my daughter. I make sure she has lots of friends to play with and she sees my cousin's children quite often. There are lots of adults who are close to us who she calls Auntie and Uncle so I don't feel she misses out on the family front.

PARENT TRAPS:
YOUR ONLY CHILD AND YOU

The special child
Each child is special but from the outside many people think that onlies are made to feel too special. In fact, I have the impression

that most parents of only children work exceptionally hard to make sure that they are not, by making her feel she is unique, extremely talented or whatever, placing extra burdens on their child.

The danger is for unfulfilled parents to project their own wishes and desires on to the child. By saying you are such a special child you are giving a covert message: *Be like I want to be. I have hidden needs I want you to satisfy.* This scenario is by no means confined to families with a single child (many a child is singled out in a larger family for special attention), but obviously it is a trap to be wary of.

Idolizing your child

Some parents simply idolize and idealize their child (or children!). The child can virtually do no wrong; she is always described in glowing terms and praised to high heaven for all her efforts, justified or not. Unfortunately the child who is the recipient of such feelings grows up thinking she has to be extraordinary to have any self-worth – she can't just be average at something, she has to be the best. Success then becomes a necessity if the child is to live up to the parents' unrealistic vision of her.

Mirror image

There is an expectation by some parents that their children will mirror both their positive and negative traits. You can hear them saying things like 'Little Johnny is no good at maths. He simply hasn't got a head for figures. He's just like me in that respect.' This can become a self-fulfilling prophecy as the child stops making any effort in maths; or he may overcompensate. It is equally damaging for the parent to assume that because he is a whiz on the computer, his child will be. The child grows up constantly struggling to excel at something for which he has neither the talent nor inclination. When this type of parent has a larger family there is more likelihood he will find a like-minded child among the brood to satisfy his need, but again at what cost to the child who may never throw off that particular yoke and explore other avenues.

Superchild syndrome

Once again this doesn't just apply to parents of onlies. There always seem to be adults who are intent on creating a superchild – one who excels at everything and is sent to extracurricular classes in music, gym, French, drama, tennis, etc., etc. This parent is in reality trying to meet her own needs: perhaps she felt she missed out as a child, always wanted to learn a musical instrument, speak another language, play tennis and so on. It is definitely not to the child's benefit to be whisked from one enriching experience to the next. A child must have time to be a child, to engage in childish things, to play with her toys and to relax in front of the television or a video from time to time. Unhappily a child who is brought up in this frenetic way is given the message that self-worth is equated with performance. For the child to be worthy of her parent's love she has to perform perfectly.

THE ONLY CHILD IN LITERATURE

The only child gets a bad press in the media, but in children's literature it's rather a different story, and there's no shortage of role models. Many authors have chosen the only child to be the central character in a book. One reason for this is that there are less children to get in the way of the plot. Another is that they can begin by focusing on one of the negative aspects of being an only child and turn it round to the child's advantage. Bridie in *Paddy's Pot of Gold* by Dick King Smith is able to see the leprechaun in her garden by virtue of the fact that she is an only child; it's one of the preconditions, along with having a hole in her boot on her birthday.

Only children are a great favourite with the master storyteller Roald Dahl. James, in *James and the Giant Peach*, an orphan victim of his two horrendous aunts, has an amazing journey across the Atlantic in the company of giant insects, and poverty-stricken Charlie inherits the chocolate factory. Classic children's literature is equally peopled by onlies. Both Mary and Colin are lonely only children in *The Secret Garden* while Little Lord Fauntleroy is the epitome of a charming, well-brought up child (a credit to his widowed – and therefore single – mother!) who wins the heart of everyone he comes into contact with, including his crotchety, snobbish old grandfather.

In traditional fairy tales, both Cinderella and Snow White are beloved only daughters who have their lives turned upside-down by a wicked step-mother but overcome all adversity, and triumph by marrying the prince in the end.

Even the Victorian novelist Charles Dickens, writing during a time when large families were almost *de rigueur*, includes many only children as his main characters; Little Nell in *The Old Curiosity Shop*, Oliver Twist, Pip and Estelle in *Great Expectations*, (he by virtue of the fact that he is brought up by his much older sister), and of course David Copperfield. Counter-examples to the popular, prejudicial model of the only child abound.

SUMMARY

How can we shed an image of only children that seems so widespread in our culture? Well, for one thing we can stop being apologetic for having one child and always talk about the very real positive aspects. The good news is that more and more people seem to be choosing to have one child – so there'll always be more converts spreading the word, and having an only child will seem just as normal as having two or more children.

Secondly we must always make sure our offspring feel good about themselves rather than negative about being an only child. What we mustn't do is make our children feel guilty. Even if, for instance, you had a very difficult birth or severe post-natal depression that put you off having another child, you shouldn't tell this to your child until she is old enough to understand. And certainly you should never blame your child's birth for things that have gone wrong in your life. Children are sensitive to feelings and emotions which might not be overtly expressed.

If we bring up our children to believe that there is nothing wrong in being an only child and that there are many positive aspects, we will be well on the way to making sure future generations see a one-child family more positively.

Part One
The Child

Chapter 3

How will being an only affect your child?

'I didn't realize there were any disadvantages until you just mentioned it!' John, a writer in his late sixties, on being asked about his experiences as an only child.

The trouble with trying to gauge how being an only will affect any child is that there is no control group by which to judge the child. No two sets of circumstances or children are ever completely the same so there's no absolute base to judge from. Even studies of twins who were separated at birth fail to come up with conclusive proof in the nurture versus nature debate. The fact that sets of twins brought up separately have married at the same time to partners of the same name can hardly be attributed to some dedicated gene that prescribes whom we will marry! Who you are is decided by everything which has happened in your life including and especially the family and environment you were born into. Change one part of the context and your whole life might turn out completely differently.

This is equally true from the parenting side of the equation. As I only have one child, I do not know what sort of mother I would be to two or three offspring. I have a daughter and am constantly making choices about the way I bring her up; would the way I brought up a son be considerably different? I would like to think that it wouldn't. I can make educated guesses about alternative scenarios but that is all. I can't know what might have been. My daughter's character and outlook on life would be different if she had one or two siblings, but who knows in what way? All we can do as parents is to attempt to give our children – with or without siblings – the best possible start in life by trying to avoid the pitfalls and learning from other people's experiences.

THE ONLY CHILD: OUTDATED IDEAS AND POPULAR STEREOTYPES

While parents get on with the job, experts grapple with our psychology, determined to find reasons for any given behaviour. The problem with a lot of past studies into the development of only children as distinct from those in larger families, however, is that they rely strongly on adult subjects (usually undergraduates, who obviously give a very subjective view), or children with behavioural problems and who have come to the psychologists' attention for that reason. These adults and children are not indicative of the population at large, and certainly not of only children in particular.

Only child, by Jill Pittkeathley and David Emerson, one of the few non-academic books on only children, shows the influence of this approach. The authors quote extensively from only children, but all of these were interviewed as adults, some of them very old, and all seemed to blame anything and everything that went even vaguely wrong in their lives onto the absence of brothers and sisters. The subtitle is 'How To Survive Being One', and that sums up its premiss: being an only child makes you different and this difference is a real handicap. This premiss is a cop-out. All sorts of problems, from being difficult to live with (how interesting that that should just be applicable to onlies!) to feeling apart and isolated, are attributed to their singular child state. I'm sure that anyone reading it would recognize many of the symptoms and problems mentioned. They are all an intrinsic part of growing up and children from two, three- or more child families may suffer just as much.

There comes a time in everyone's life when you have to stop blaming your parents, family, school and upbringing or whatever else, and take responsibility for the way you are and try to effect changes if necessary. This is what being a mature adult is all about.

These studies have to be looked at very carefully, taking this sort of bias into consideration. Another factor to be born in mind when reviewing research is that situations and considerations that were applicable to children twenty or more years ago are not necessarily relevant today. Fashions in childcare change. Mother and toddler groups, preschool playgroups and nurseries now abound, when thirty or more years ago they were virtually non-existent. As I show throughout Part One, changing assumptions of this kind can be very beneficial for your only child.

The popular view of only children as expressed by these authors and their interviewees is that they are immature and have particularly undesirable traits especially in how they relate to other people. In the past psychologists have paid a lot of attention to this and have given credence to the theory that the only child is disadvantaged, but more recent studies generally vindicate the only child, who is no more likely to behave in socially unacceptable ways than anyone else is.

THE ONLY AS A YOUNG ADULT: MODERN RESEARCH

The results from Project Talent, carried out by John G. Clandy and quoted in *The Single Child Family*, show that in cognitive ability and intellect only children were equal to and perhaps slightly superior to children with siblings. There were no significant differences or trends in terms of calmness, impulsiveness, leadership, self-control and vitality. Onlies as young children were seen as more cultured, mature, socially sensitive and tidy, with more adult characteristics, whereas children with siblings were on the whole more sociable.

Again this is a generalization: there will always be only children who act more childishly, are less cultured, socially sensitive and tidy and are more sociable than children with siblings. The main feature of this study which we should underline and point out to

33

all those who condemn only children is that there were no appreciable differences in many areas between them and children with siblings.

There is also research from America that support this. 'Without siblings: The consequences in adult life of having been an only child', which is in *The Single Child Family* (1984), found there was no evidence of any negative consequences for onlies compared to non-onlies in patterns of behaviour in adult life.

Intelligence

All sorts of factors combine to influence the development of intelligence in a child, including experience within the family. The studies, which are quoted throughout this book have shown that only children do seem to be intelligent high-achievers but this is also true of the older sibling (where the children are less than 6 years apart) in two-child families. The studies deal in statistics and averages, and it doesn't mean that every only child or the older of two children is or will be slightly more intelligent. Statistically children from small families fare better than those from large families but there will always be very able and intelligent children born into larger families just as there are always onlies and elder children who have learning difficulties. What is important is the potential each child is born with and the way that potential is or isn't brought to fruition.

It has been argued by psychologists including D. Winnicott that family size affects intelligence in that having a younger sibling gives an older child the opportunity to tutor, and tutoring a younger sibling benefits both the older and younger child's intellectual development. This is open to discussion, and it is only one factor in a child's development; but if you think the tutoring aspect is important it is comparatively easy to arrange for your child to play with a younger one from time to time – most children do so anyway.

Only children gain because very often parents can devote more time to them, especially in supervising homework, hearing them read and generally stimulating them.

Motivation

> *Being an only child . . . I became very self-motivated, very self-reliant . . . I remember whole weekends when I wouldn't see another kid and was happy to play with my train set or cricket with my dad. You get a better imagination.* Noel Edmonds

Only children automatically have what every child needs – a chance to be on their own. This allows them time to improve their powers of concentration and allows for the single-minded attention which is vital for their development. This helps in problem solving, by having the time to search for new ways to do things without having siblings interfering and interrupting. In this way the child gains independence and her self-confidence grows.

With this comes the knowledge that being alone can be fun and rewarding, something everyone can benefit from. The child playing on her own has a chance to be her own boss, an opportunity to be fully in control. Adults who have experienced this and achieved this in childhood jealously guard time on their own once they are grown up, as you will see from various comments in this book as well as this one from John, a lecturer married with two children.

> *I feel feel extremely self-reliant, seldom if ever bored and quite at ease with my own company. I remember saying at quite a young age that I thought it was usually easier to go out and find company than to find solitude. To some extent I remain a fairly solitary type.*

Achievement

First-born and only children tend to perform better academically. Onlies compare favourably to people from larger families. The motivation to achieve has been thought to originate in the high standards for mature behaviour that parents impose on their child at a relatively early age; it seems particularly true for standards in politeness and table manners.

The exaggerated amount of parental attention and encouragement to achieve onlies may receive can have negative aspects (the child may feel there is too much pressure on her to achieve), but a desire to obtain the maximum possible in education is instilled and therefore onlies may tend to gravitate towards a more socially prestigious occupation.

> *I did not have any friends of my own age and compensated by having imaginary friends and making up stories . . . If I'd had millions of friends and Brownies and playgroups to go to, like my kids have, and not the rather curious relationships I had, I would not have been a writer. In that way my childhood was of inestimable value.* Susan Hill, novelist

Studies have revealed that only children tend to have a greater interest in physical science, biological science, music, computers and literary occupations, while non-onlies tend to favour sports, hunting and fishing, office work, mechanical and technical skilled trades and labour. No difference was found between the number of onlies and non-onlies choosing to work in public service, social science, the arts, business management, sales and farming.

One difference which did emerge was that only children are less likely to work and earn money while still at school, which might of course be due to the fact that there is less economic need to do so in a smaller family. Another was that only children tended to have more definite career plans at an earlier age. Naomi, a mother of an only daughter, has very definite and positive views of onlies in the work place.

> *I work with quite a lot of other people who are onlies and I have lots of friends who are also only children. I think what I find attractive about them is their self-sufficiency and directness. They are also happy in their own company. I think this applies to me as well. I like to be in control at work. Delegation is one thing, sharing the role is quite another!*

Behaviour

Only and first born children often expect other people to comfort them during stress, perhaps because their mothers responded more promptly to their cries and demands as babies. Later born children may have been left to cry for longer, and therefore learned not to expect immediate attention, and as young children may have learned to sort things out for themselves; certainly the larger the family the more likely it becomes that children at some times will be left very much to their own devices.

In earlier studies and research of previous generations only children were compared with children who have one sibling or more and were found to belong to fewer organizations; they reported having fewer friends and visiting friends and relatives less often. They also reported a less intense social life, and this fits with the accounts of older onlies interviewed for his book. Like John, or Noel Edmonds, the only children who were studied do not appear to have suffered as a result of this; more importantly, they do not see themselves as missing out.

Ann Laybourn, of the Centre for the Study of the Child and Society at the University of Glasgow, analysed information from the National Child Development Study (a long term research project monitoring children born between 3–9 March 1958 who were questioned at ages 7, 11, 16, 23 and 33). Her findings agreed with other recent research, that there are few significant personality differences between only and one-sibling children, but that both children were different from those from larger families. Her conclusion is that only children turn out more like than unlike children with siblings in terms of personality and behaviour.

Family life

Only children often have an uninterrupted relationship with their parents and as a result frequently become more adult-orientated. Several investigations suggest that the only child has a special relationship with her parents. There is more parent–child inter-action than among first and later born children and a study in 1978 (*Adolescents' perceptions of parental affection: an investigation of only child vs first borns*, Journal of Population: Behaviour, Social & Environmental Issues) found that only children perceived themselves as having more affectionate relationships with their parents than first-borns. Naomi found this to be true.

I had and continue to have a very good relationship with my parents. I enjoyed a very nice childhood and never felt the slightest bit deprived of siblings. My mother always said it wasn't a bundle of laughs having siblings and I believed her. I don't find sharing friends, my home or my possessions difficult, I like sharing what I have but sharing parents is a very difficult concept for me.

It is a generally held view of only children that they are less cooperative in social situations. However, conclusions from research show that only children are more likely to make cooperative rather than competitive moves in games. This means that they probably fare better in team games rather than in competitive sports.

Marriage and children

Four factors were revealed in studies begun in the 1960s and followed up when the interviewees were twenty-nine.

Only children expect to but do not in fact marry at a later age; they expect to and do in fact have fewer children; spouses of only children are more educated but do not differ in age to spouses of non-onlies; onlies are less likely to be divorced at twenty-nine.

Health-related concerns

There is no appreciable long-term difference between only children and those with siblings in relation to matters of both physical and mental heath. Only children are no more likely to become anxious, neurotic or be prone to phobias than any other child. There is no evidence either to suggest that parents of only children are more likely to wrap their children in cotton wool and rush them to a doctor at the first sign of a sneeze.

One area of the National Child Development Study considered by Ann Laybourn that did show a difference between only children and those with siblings was that of being overweight. At ages seven and twenty-three there was no significant difference between the number of onlies and non-onlies who were over-weight. However at eleven 18 per cent of onlies compared with 9 per cent of non-onlies were overweight. This had fallen at sixteen to 12 per cent of onlies and 8 per cent of children with one sibling. This may tie in with the fact that at eleven only children were statistically slightly more likely to be engaged in indoor activities than outdoor ones.

The problem of children being overweight may be due to fattening foods and lack of exercise; some families see certain foods as treats and perhaps overcompensate with them. Not all only children suffer from this and it also depends on the type of family you come from. Overindulgence can be a parent trap: see page 41.

PARENT TRAPS
Too much stimulation

The temptation for parents with one child is to give her too much stimulation. This is done in a variety of ways and usually with the best of intentions. Most parents would give anything for their children; many make huge sacrifices that their children only become aware of when they are adults and have a child themselves, as one only child remembered: 'We were not very well off but I had everything I needed; it was my mother who went without the new winter coat so that I didn't suffer in any way.'

With only one child to provide for, parents can often indulge him not only with material possessions but also with hobbies he is allowed to pick up (and sometimes drop). However most parents are aware of the problems, a fact reflected in one eleven-year-old's experience. 'My parents do buy me a lot of books but I always have to read one before they buy the next one.'

Overstimulation is the most important negative aspect of having too much. It can be anything from a room full of educational toys to extracurricular classes in every imaginable subject. What all children need more than anything is the chance to be and act like children, and that applies across the board to everyone. The oldest child in a family who is put upon to look after his younger siblings and continually asked to do jobs around the house is equally missing out on his childhood.

However educationally sound and enriching it is to offer a variety of experiences, a child should also learn perseverance and not flirt with hobbies and interests because they are readily available. This is one pitfall Joanne is wary of.

I'm really aware of how much children have enthusiasms for things – like wanting to play a musical instrument, then wanting

*to drop say the violin and take up the trumpet. I certainly want my
child to have a range of experiences but I don't think she should
become a dilettante. When she wanted to give up the violin (an
instrument she had chosen to learn) we came to an agreement that
she would take a first exam and then if she wanted to give it up she
could. She hasn't taken the exam yet but the chances are that now
she is becoming so much more proficient at playing she will be less
likely to give it up. I think that applies to most things. There's a
learning curve and you have to get to a certain point before you
can really make an informed decision about whether you like it
enough to continue or not.*

Too much adult intervention

One trap parents of small or large families can fall into is to
interrupt their child's play or intervene in his conversations.
Children need to think and act for themselves (as long as they
are not placing themselves in any danger) and they need to know
that their thoughts or actions are worthy ones. If you constantly
interrupt or speak for your child she will get the message that her
opinion doesn't count. In the extreme she may begin to believe
she doesn't amount to much.

Do you intervene too much?

Do you find yourself:
- always prompting your child when she's asked a question?
- finishing her sentence?
- repeating the question perhaps in a different way?
- answering for her?
- interrupting a conversation to correct her?

If your answer is yes to any of these, take a moment to think
about why you intervene. Don't you trust her to give a good
account of herself? This is the message your intervention is
giving to your child. Give your child time to answer for herself
and allow her to say things like, 'I don't know,' even when you
know perfectly well that she does! Respect her silences or the
way she wishes to express himself as long as it isn't insulting or
disrespectful.

Overindulgence

The popular myth of the only child is that he gets everything he wants: the parents overindulge their only child, buying him presents instead of presenting him with what they are really after, a baby brother or sister! This is often far from the truth as Emma, an adult only, confirmed: 'I had everything I needed but not necessarily everything I wanted.'

Parents of onlies can actually stray in the opposite direction. I remember my daughter's first Christmas when I suddenly realized that I'd bought far more presents for my nephew than I had my daughter. I'm also careful not to give into my daughter's requests to buy things when we go shopping, whether or not I can afford them. However, it was a real eye-opener going out twice one weekend with a family who have three children. On the Saturday the mother explained that they always bought a 'pocket-money toy' at the weekend. As my daughter had some birthday money to spend I agreed but was surprised to see that their toys were all in the region of five pounds. We went out with the father the following day and the same thing occurred: he bought them all presents costing five or six pounds. By that time, having bought Olivia something for a pound, I was feeling somewhat like Scrooge before his conversion! But overdulgence can lead to severe problems. See pages 51–2.

SUMMARY

While there is some slight statistical evidence to suggest differences between only children and those with siblings in some respects, being the single child in a family need have no detrimental effect and may have various positive ones.

Chapter 4
Helping your child to make friends

CHILDREN NEED friends, and only children are no exception – in fact it's even more important for them. Some friendships begun in childhood endure for a lifetime, some don't last as long as the school term and while some children take the ebb and flow of friendships in their stride, others are heartbroken when a cherished friend deserts them.

Just as children need friends it is equally true that no parent can ever be a substitute playmate however happy you are at playing together. No matter how well-intentioned you are, you just can't play the right games! You should play with your child, but you should make sure this is only a small proportion of her playtime. Children playing together work out all sorts of problems, try new skills and sample new roles, and the last thing they need is an adult interfering, directing the action and excelling at everything.

THE FIRST STEPS
One way of ensuring your child has lots of friends is to make sure you do. Children follow a parent's example, so if they're used to you having friends around and visiting other homes they'll follow suit. If you are shy yourself then you will really have to make an extra effort on your child's behalf. A shy father, especially one who is bringing up a baby alone, should consult his health visitor about any groups which welcome fathers. In becoming a regular visitor to the baby clinic, for example, they may gain confidence about being with their baby in public. Such fathers may find coping with a baby difficult but

they may find that other mothers will offer advice and moral support. The important thing is not to turn down offers of help out of hand – all parents need a helping hand sometimes.

When a child is very young the first friends will probably come from any antenatal group you belonged to during pregnancy. Baby clinics, churches and other organizations often run mother and baby or mother and toddler groups and these are an essential element of your child's social life.

Even quite small children benefit from having little friends. They might not actually play together but they will interact and get used to other children's company and become used to sharing space and toys. At this stage parents come too so it's more bearable if you actually get on with them or have interests in common. As children get older and are dropped off to play, it really doesn't matter what your feelings are about the other parents (assuming their behaviour is acceptable and their home is safe), as long as your children get on and play happily together.

There is one proviso here: I would never feel happy sending a young child off to play in a house I hadn't visited. People's standards vary tremendously: while your house might be geared to the demands of a small, inquisitive child with safety locks everywhere, stair gates and electric-socket covers, another home might have none of these. While their child has grown up with this, yours has not and therefore could be at risk from injury. It's worth satisfying yourself on a few points before letting your child visit another home without you.

Make visits safe
- Have you visited the home?
- Are the safety provisions adequate?
- Do the parents smoke?
- If so is this in a room away from the children?
- Are any animals kept out of the way?
- Are the adults aware of any prohibitions, e.g. sweets or sweet drinks?
- Do you have their phone number in case you need it?
- Do they have yours?

As your child gets older, you won't feel you have to be quite so careful and you'll probably find that your child, having absorbed your ideas on safety, hygiene and house rules, will observe these in somebody else's home.

EXTENDING YOUR SOCIAL CIRCLE

As your child grows older, encourage her to develop a range of interests. Even for preschool children there is a whole host of activities available, from mini-gym/tumble tots to French clubs, from small music groups to dance classes, and most of them will probably require a certain amount of parental supervision or participation. As children get older they can join in more formally organized activities like the Beavers, Cubs and Scouts and Rainbows, Brownies and Guides, the church choir, the football club, the chess club, after-school activities or whatever they fancy. That is not to say that I believe every moment of a child's life should be planned and catered for, but a healthy balance between being at home and out engaged in some activity with other children is necessary and desirable.

One of the criticisms aimed at the parents of only children is that that child has to be everything. They have, metaphorically speaking, put all their eggs in one basket, so the child has to be all things – the artist, the singer, the intelligent one, the athlete. In larger families, so the argument goes, there is less pressure on individual children. However they do tend to get cast in a role: the pretty one, the creative one, the musician, the baby of the family. These roles are often restrictive and restricting and are hard to break out of: the 'pretty' one might have an amazing intellect that is never acknowledged, the 'artist' might also be a whiz on computers. In this light I think the only child has more going for her: she gets to try out lots of different things and is never so narrowly labelled, as one mother explains.

In my family I was the 'clever' one. My sister was the pretty one who went to dance classes. I loved dancing but never got the opportunity to join a class even though I did ask my parents. I'm not saying it would have made an enormous difference to my life but it would have been a nice alternative to studying. My sister did take up dancing for a while but she in fact discovered a talent for business that might have been helped by more attention to her more formal education.

I made a conscious decision to have one child and I'm determined he should try out as many things as he can, to gain as much experience of life. To make choices from an informed viewpoint. However, I don't just let him pick up and drop activities on a whim. I make sure he gives everything a good try. For instance, he decided he didn't like swimming and I can understand that, not being a great swimmer myself. However I pointed out that swimming was a necessary skill – he could drown if he fell out of a fishing boat or whatever – and we agreed that once he reached a certain competence, say being able to swim twenty-five metres, he would be able to give up the swimming classes.'

Children love accumulating badges and certificates and even comparatively young ones enjoy working towards goals. Pre-school children benefit from situations where they have to sit still and pay attention for short periods: this is good preparation for the classroom and children do need to be able to listen and follow instructions. Once they have acquired certain skills needed for an activity they might find they enjoy it more and want to continue with it. Children who are good at a sport or who have acquired a skill often find their popularity increases along with their self-esteem. Everyone wants the boy who is good at football on their side. A child who is an ace at general knowledge will be a welcomed member of any team. Encourage any talent your child has but remember to stress the importance of modesty: nobody likes a braggart even if he is as good as he says he is (see Chapter Five, Teaching your child social skills).

BEING PART OF A GROUP

Children constantly amaze me by their need to conform to the norms of their peer group. An adult will sometimes find this frustrating, at other times annoying. When there is a conflict between the standards and mores of the family and the play-ground rules and use of vernacular, it is helpful for the child if you explain that what is acceptable behaviour in one area of his life isn't in another. Slang expressions and sloppy speech, for instance, can drive parents up the wall: explain that the language he uses with his friends is fine in the playground but shouldn't be used in the classroom or at home. My own daughter grasped this idea very quickly and then I think we both relaxed a bit more.

The preschool years

During the first years of life, children seem relatively unaffected by the pressures exerted by a peer group. Often this is confined to wanting to own the same toys as someone else. Or preferring to wear leggings because Rosie at nursery does. However there does come a time that any parent dreads – the unsavoury influence of another child on your little darling! For a child who attends a playgroup, nursery, one o'clock club or just mixes with other children is bound to come home at some stage or another delighted with the new word she has learned – and it's usually a word guaranteed to make you cringe with embarrassment when it's used in front of the in-laws!

School age

School makes an amazing impact on a child's life. Peer pressure to conform is rife and a child who is perceived as different in any way can be singled out for teasing at best, bullying at worst (see page 00). Children meet a whole spectrum of new people from the staff to pupils and may go through some trying phases, asserting their own personality before settling down. Friendships need to be handled sensitively – never express disapproval of another child. This is based on your own prejudices and feelings. What you can say is that you don't like the way so and so behaves (if the behaviour is indeed unacceptable to you) but try to be as non-judgemental as you would like others to be towards you and your family. Your own child will soon be side-lined if he goes to school saying, 'My mummy doesn't like the way you speak,' or whatever.

The importance of casual acquaintances

Another negative aspect of an only child, according to some child experts, is that children with siblings tend to get to know their brother's or sister's friends on a more informal, relaxed basis and so broaden their circle of acquaintances; an only child lacking these, may tend to be more intense and perhaps a little exclusive in friendships. This does not have to be the case and the situation varies more with the sociability of the family than the number of children in it.

In my own experience, intense and exclusive friendships can evolve with any child, with or without siblings. These friendships are very important and often very rewarding, but do mean that a child can end up on her own in the playground, or has no one to sit next to at lunchtime, if her special friend is away from school. An obvious solution to this is to encourage your child to play with a wider group of children at school and to supply casual acquaintances. These can be found by joining clubs and becoming part of a group. I am continually astonished at how many children my own daughter seems to know. She meets some through swimming lessons, others through the French classes I run, even more at Sports Experience, a school vacation activity centre, and through friends of friends.

It takes a bit of effort on the parents' part to extend your child's range of friends but it's well worth it. One way is to talk to parents you meet when dropping your child at school and invite their children round to play. For parents who work this is more difficult but more and more working parents are sending notes into school to invite a child round to play at the weekend or during a school holiday. If you do this, make the invitation very clear, stating the time you expect the child, what time he or she is to be collected and whether the invitation includes a meal. It's surprising how often plans go awry because an invitation isn't explicit.

The importance of continuity

A corollary of the importance of casual acquaintances is an emphasis on continuity in a child's life, especially with friendships. Children who have been important to each other at nursery or bosom pals at play group should not be dropped as soon as the child starts school or a new group. New friends will come along but it's always nice to relax with someone you've known for a long time, as we adults know. If your child is going to attend a school away from his other friends make a point of keeping in touch (until they are old enough to do it for themselves, and then watch the phone bill!) and arrange for your child to play with his friends every so often after school or at weekends. Continuity helps make transitions easier and you may find that your child relaxes more with a child she isn't in competition with in the classroom.

Losing friends

Some children shrug off the end of a friendship like an old coat that doesn't fit any more. Others are heartbroken when a friend deserts them or circumstances dictate that they won't see each other again. I can still remember sobbing all the way home from primary school when my best friend at that time told me she didn't like me any more. My own daughter was clearly upset when a close friend from nursery moved away – the parents didn't give me their new address so there was no way we could contact them. Parents should be sensitive to a child's feelings, careful not to underestimate the power of childhood friendships or the grief of losing a friend their child may experience.

UNPOPULARITY

What do you do if your child is unpopular? I think it's possibly one of the hardest things a parent has to cope with. No one likes to think that their own flesh and blood has few friends and is basically lonely.

So how do you find out if your child is on the sidelines? One way is to ask her to draw a picture of the school playground or some sort of group activity in which she takes part. Even a limited amount of artistic prowess can be revealing, as Julie found out.

I was really worried about Darren. Whenever I asked him who he played with at school he'd mutter, 'nobody' or just clam up. One day we were drawing together and I suggested we both draw pictures of the school. I drew him in the middle of a game surrounded by other children. His picture showed him on one side of the playground, on his own, while everyone else was involved in something on the other side. When he saw my picture he was quite emphatic that my portrait of him wasn't him. I realized how lonely he must feel and took steps to help him make friends.

Is your child lonely?

She is if a few of these statements apply. She . . .

- mentions few friends at school
- rarely asks to have someone home to play
- is rarely invited to others' houses to play
- is rather timid
- dislikes team sports
- has something which marks her as different to others: for instance stammers, wears a brace, or limps

---

Dealing with unpopularity

You can help by

- organizing a group activity (see below)
- encouraging social skills (see Chapter Five)
- giving her something to play with during break times: a skipping rope, ball or some jacks may encourage other children to join her
- teach her to laugh at teasing
- reduce differences: you can't change some things but you can, for instance make sure she's wearing the same sort of clothes – for boys wearing short trousers when no one else is can be excruciatingly embarrassing; children are amazing conformists!
- boost her self-esteem (see Chapter Eight)
- encourage a talent, sport or aptitude: how many of our comedians and comic writers were made fun of in the playground and won friends over by making them laugh?

Parties, as many adults appreciate, are a great way of extending your social circle. You don't have to spend a lot of money and can keep refreshments simple. Fancy-dress parties are usually a great success. But you don't really have to go to such lengths – you can't be organizing parties all the time – so why not introduce the idea of theme teas? Just invite two or more children and explain the idea. Hallowe'en and pancake parties are self-explanatory and you can make appropriate food. If your family celebrates other festivals like Hanukkah, Diwali or Chinese New Year you could invite some other children who are perhaps unfamiliar with the occasion to share your festivities. But don't wait for a festival – make one up. All you need is a little time, imagination and preparation. But do involve the children as much as you can so that the preparation is all part of the fun.

Ideas for theme teas

- Hallowe'en
- pancake party
- dressing up as a favourite TV or film character
- The Mad Hatter's Tea Party
- ethnic and international food

You might also like to include another child when you go to the theatre or cinema – many have reduced family tickets so the cost of an extra child is minimal. Or perhaps you're involved in a sport that might interest your child's classmate? Trips to the park or playground, swimming pool or leisure centre are always popular, just as making a tent in the back garden and leaving the children to play is a great favourite.

Having it all!

Just as children like conformity, wearing the same clothes and shoes as their friends so too they will find it easier to make friends if they are not overindulged. If you have a tendency to indulge your child, think again. A child who has too many toys or too much pocket money can find herself isolated from other children.

When you only have one child it is often easier both financially and emotionally to give what they ask for. However aiming for a more balanced upbringing is more appropriate as Emma said: 'I had everything I needed but not necessarily everything I wanted.'

No one gets everything they want in life so it's better not to think that you do as a child. As one mother of an only said: 'Often I don't buy things for her when she asks. I can usually afford it but that's not the point. I don't want to spoil her. Sometimes I'm probably harder on her than a parent of more than one child would be.'

BULLYING

Children who are spoilt rotten often resort to bullying. So do those who are bullied themselves or are abused at home. Bullying can include anything from name calling to physical abuse and none of it should be tolerated. Here is one mother's experience of incipient bullying.

When my daughter first started school she immediately made friends with another little girl, who was obviously used to getting everything her own way. They are both only children but the other child had been seriously ill – though had completely recovered – and it seemed she had really been overindulged. At school, if she didn't like my child's picture she would scribble over it. If my daughter wore her hair in plaits and the other didn't approve she would pull them out. I felt quite cross with Claire for not sticking up for herself. I did see the teacher but she wasn't particularly sympathetic, so I decided on my own course of action. I invited some other children in her class – individually – to have tea with Claire after school and this worked really well. Being friends with the other children meant Claire wasn't so dependent on this bullying girl and these other friends in turn supported Claire and gave her the confidence to say no when she wanted to. The other girl couldn't take over the whole group.

Is your child being bullied?

Children rarely come straight out and say they are being bullied, and sometimes they make all sorts of excuses for any change in behaviour or routine. They may suddenly want you to walk or drive them to school, for example, or they may ask for extra pocket money if bullies are stealing from them or are asking for 'protection money' (as horrifying as this seems). If you're worried that your child is being bullied, a quiet word with the teacher may be all that's needed but in more extreme cases, if the problem is not being dealt with (or even acknowledged, which is even more frustrating for the child and parent alike!), you might have to consult the head teacher and governors.

Is your child being bullied?

Any one or a combination of the following may mean your child is the victim of bullying. Has he:

- started wetting the bed?
- felt ill before going to school?
- become more withdrawn and lacking in confidence?
- begun doing poorly in school work?
- begun to cry himself to sleep?
- begun to have disturbed nights or nightmares?
- asked to change from packed lunches or school dinners?
- suddenly refused to go into the playground without you?
- suddenly not wanted you in the playground?
- come home with clothes or books torn or destroyed?
- acquired unexplained scratches or bruises?

How to help your child if bullied

KIDSCAPE is a national charity which teaches children about personal safety (see the appendix on Useful Addresses for further information). It has produced these pointers on how to support your child:

- keep telling your child you love him very much and are 100 per cent on his side
- reassure him that the bullying is not his fault

- explain that reacting to bullies by crying or becoming upset only encourages them
- practise assertiveness techniques with him – like saying 'No' very firmly and walking away from a bully
- help him to think up simple responses to the bully's most frequent taunts – it helps to have a reply prepared
- try to minimize opportunities for bullying: don't take valuable possessions to school, don't be the last person in a changing room, don't linger alone in corridors – there's safety in numbers
- if the bully threatens your child to get money or possessions, tell him that they should give up whatever the bully wants. Keeping safe is more important than keeping possessions
- make time to sit down and talk to your child – encourage him to tell you how he feels: discuss his ideas and feelings
- praise him whenever they accomplish something or whenever he behaves well
- give him responsibilities – this helps to make him feel valued and important

Above all, make sure your child feels he has your love and support by telling him and showing him he is lovable and loved. Never blame your child or tell him to hit back or kick harder than his aggressor. This is all counter-productive. If necessary, help him with social skills (see Chapter Five) and his social life (see above) and build up his self-esteem (see Chapter Eight).

Is your child a bully?

It is sometimes very difficult for a parent to accept that her own child is a bully. Children learn through experience and often reflect in their own behaviour the way they are themselves being treated. If your child is behaving in an overbearing way it may mean you have to change the way you're reacting to her: if you hit her you're passing on the message that hitting is OK, and the same goes for verbal abuse; to shout and scream at your child implies that this is reasonable behaviour for her to emulate.

A prime example of this was something I overheard in a playground when a mother was scolding a child for bullying a classmate: 'If you do that again you'll feel my foot on your backside, you little . . .' The parent here was as guilty as her daughter. How could the little girl learn that it's wrong to bully and hurt anyone younger, smaller or less confident than herself, if she is being bullied by her parent – someone who is older, bigger and more confident?

Is your child a bully?

If four or more of these statements apply to your child she could be a bully. The higher the score over four, the higher the risk. My child . . .

- is bigger than her peer group
- wants her own way all the time
- wants to be the centre of attention
- is frequently smacked when naughty
- is often in trouble
- disobeys adults
- doesn't work well at school
- has very few close friends

How to help the bullying child

If you discover or suspect your child is a bully, there are several things you can do. First of all, however upset you feel, try to stay calm and not angry and defensive. Your child needs your help and support, not your condemnation at this point. If the bullying is happening at school, make an appointment to see the class teacher or the head to discuss the matter; find out what your child has been accused of and if she has behaved like this on other occasions. Listen carefully and if it helps you, make notes. Talk to other parents and staff, such as dinner ladies and support staff. Try not to be confrontational – it doesn't help and may make people less inclined to assist you. Once you have all the facts you can talk to your child about the problem.

KIDSCAPE recommends the following thirteen point programme for helping a child who bullies.

- see if she has any ideas about why she bullies and what she thinks might help her stop
- reassure your child that you still love her – it's her behaviour you don't like but you will work with her to help change this
- find out if there is something in particular which is troubling her and try to sort it out
- work out a way for her to make amends for the bullying
- set up some sort of reward for good behaviour
- set limits. Stop any show of aggression immediately and help her find other non-aggressive ways of reacting
- if your child bullies when faced with certain situations, help her work out and practise alternative ways of behaving
- explain that getting away from the situation where she can feel herself losing her temper, or things are getting out of hand, is not weakness. It is a sensible way of ensuring that the situation doesn't get worse
- teach your child the difference between assertive behaviour and aggressive behaviour
- praise your child when she does things well. Create opportunities for her to shine
- talk to the school staff. Explain that your child is making an effort to change her behaviour. Ask what ideas they have to help. It might be helpful for you and your child to talk to an educational psychologist. Ask the school to arrange this
- talk to the staff about setting realistic goals for your child – don't expect too much too soon – and about rewarding her when she achieves one of these goals.

Ask if the school can provide a room where the child can go if she feels she needs time to 'cool off'

- other children may deliberately provoke a bully, especially if they think the bully is trying to reform. Explain to your child that she may be taunted and provoked but she should try not to respond aggressively. She should walk quickly away if they think someone is trying to pick a fight.

The KIDSCAPE *You Can Beat Bullying!* booklet (available from the charity when you send a stamped, self addressed envelope) has more suggestions for older children and young people.

Parent traps

Don't:

- try to be a substitute playmate for your child
- buy too many toys – toys cannot replace another child's company
- give too much pocket money – it may set your child apart and make others envious
- try to buy friends with treats that other parents might not be able or willing to match – your child might not be invited back
- consistently organize your child's games instead of letting him get on with it himself

Summary

All children need to learn how to make friends and how to react in a friendly way. This is imperative for an only child. Friendships have to be worked at and initially parents are the ones who have to do all the organizing of visits. However, a happy, confident child will soon be making her own friends and have an active social circle. If this is not true for your child, follow the advice in this chapter and the others in Part One, and take a leading role until your child feels happy to do so.

Chapter 5
Teaching your child social skills

P<small>ARENTS</small> are teachers to their child from the moment of birth and other family members and childcarers all contribute to the socialization process. Good manners are never a hindrance and a child who requests things politely and persuasively and always says please and thank you will have a head start over a child who makes demands and has a horror of saying please or thank you.

T<small>HE</small> IMPORTANCE OF SOCIAL SKILLS

Children with poor social skills tend to do less well at school, have less friends and may become bullies if allowed to continue antisocial behaviour unchecked. Often a child has had no limits imposed, and so doesn't realize her behaviour is unacceptable. For instance, a child who is allowed to interrupt other people, impose her will and behave aggressively at home (or has this behaviour as her role model from parents) will assume this type of conduct is also suitable at school and will be in for a rude awakening, as one mother found.

> I was really fed up with the teacher my son had last year and I'm worried about how he's going to get on with his new teacher this year. He's already got a bit of a reputation. I always seem to be up the school about something. The trouble is he always speaks his mind. He's very bright and when he's finished his work in class he gets up and talks to people. The teacher accuses me of spending too much time with him – I ask

*you, you can't win. I told the teacher she should get on with it
and instil a bit more discipline . . .*

To any teachers reading this, the mother and child must sound like the family from hell. In fact the child had a reputation for being something of a playground bully. He was also incapable of being quiet when asked and frequently interrupted other children's work. He couldn't wait for his turn at something and therefore tried to commandeer the computer or a piece of apparatus. As a result of all this he was often excluded from the classroom.

The mother's whole stance was aggressive. She never listened properly to what the school was trying to convey to her and was obviously passing this conduct on to her son.

Children learn by example: it's generally true that loud, aggressive parents produce loud, aggressive children while polite, caring parents foster polite, caring children.

Is your child prone to frustration?
Does she:
- cry easily in frustration?
- get agitated easily?
- ask others for help?
- give up easily?
- lack perseverance and persistence?

Is your child self-centred?
Watch out for the warning signs! Does she:

- always want to enjoy things for herself?
- fail to share things with other children?
- do as she likes?
- act according to her own interest?

A child constructs the foundations for social skills during the first three years of her life. From the moment she is born a baby is picking up messages from those around her and learning to make sense of them. An infant who smiles at her parent and sees that face smile back at her already feels that she has some control in a brief social exchange. Setting a good example can't begin too early.

How to encourage social skills

- Make positive remarks
- Show her how to talk and actively listen
- Show her how to include others
- Teach her to share
- Take turns with her
- Allow her to take responsibility for some things
- Allow her to help you and others
- Help her to understand how others feel
- Encourage modesty
- Show her how to win and lose
- Help her cope with anger
- Demonstrate self-control

Make positive remarks

A child who has poor social skills often feels that there is something about herself that is not quite right, that she doesn't look right, so make sure you tell her positive things about her appearance and behaviour, at the same time taking care not to suggest that how people look is of paramount importance. Compliments help to boost self-esteem.

Show her how to talk and actively listen

Recent commentators have suggested that we are in danger of breeding a nation of grunters. Our children, they say, have not acquired the art of polite conversation; their language skills are limited and so therefore are their social skills. Many social skills depend on being able to convey thoughtfulness, feeling and emotion through language. If a child only hears orders bellowed at him sometimes from another room in the house, how is he supposed to respond but by bellowing back?

Mealtimes are important social occasions which, unfortunately, have had their significance eroded. While the demands of increasingly busy lives, especially where both parents work, mean that it may not always be feasible for a family to sit round a table together for every meal, it is imperative that some meals become sacrosanct to the family. Maybe you always breakfast together or maybe Saturday lunchtimes are special in your household. Whatever you opt for a meal together as a family should be a time for catching up with each other's lives and commenting on interesting things that have happened during the day or week. It's an ideal time for learning communication skills.

If all meals are eaten 'on the hoof' or from a tray in front of the television there is no chance for any communication beyond 'pass the salt'. Whereas it can be fun to share a meal and a favourite TV programme from time to time, when it becomes a habit social interaction decreases and social skills suffer.

What we eat and the way in which we eat it varies from family to family, from culture to culture and from one social group to another, but it is important that children grow up learning what is generally considered to be acceptable behaviour and good table manners within the community. A child who is allowed to dip fingers into food others are about to eat, for instance, is being shown no favours. At school or at birthday parties or tea at friends' homes that child's manners will not be tolerated by either adults or children, as one parent noted.

One party I was at a four-year-old picked at all the fruit he was being offered, then selected the biggest strawberry, bit into it then spat it out into the fruit bowl. It was the other children who were most appalled. And no, that child wasn't an only.

If anything I believe only children have a definite edge over children with siblings. Higher standards are normally expected of them and as parents have only one child to oversee, he usually gets more direct input and less distraction. Mealtimes among families with more than one child are often reduced to acting by the lowest common denominator. That is one child will get away with some misdemeanour because another one is being admonished for doing something worse.

However some parents, of onlies or siblings, do baby their offspring at mealtimes, only ever offering 'children's' food and not worrying if they eat with their mouth open, speak with a full mouth and so on. These children will need to brush up their table manners before they're invited out!

Show her how to include others

Learning to include someone who is left out is very important. You'll often find that one child is constantly left out in a play situation – for a variety of reasons; sometimes she is just too timid to ask to join in. Your child should learn to be aware of this and should be encouraged to think about how she would feel in that situation. From the age of six or so children can become quite adept at putting themselves in someone else's shoes and this helps to make them more sensitive to other children's needs.

Teach her to share

All children have to learn to share and the younger the child the less able she is to do this. To an eighteen-month-old, being asked to share a toy is like giving it away. They haven't enough practice to know that shared toys are then returned.

People assume that a child who has no siblings is less able and likely to be able to share. That is not necessarily so, as many parents' experience will testify. A child who is constantly told to share his most treasured possessions with his younger brother or sister may grow resentful and angry. A first child presented with a sibling suddenly has to share his home, his parents, often his bedroom, his grandparents and so on, all at once. It's a hard lesson to learn. An only child who learns to share when other children come to play may feel less resentful and happier to oblige – knowing that it's only for a short while!

One problem which often arises when other children come to play, and this applies equally to children with siblings, is that there is a special toy which has an enormous significance to a particular child and there is no way she is going to share it under any circumstance. In this case it's better to put the toy safely away until the visit is over.

As children grow older and are more used to sharing they don't seem to be quite so affected by special toys. In fact they are probably eager to show them off and play with them cooperatively.

Take turns with her

One of the most important social skills needed throughout life is the ability to take turns. Just think of the people you know who dominate the conversation or who clam up and offer very little to another person. They refuse, in effect, to take their turn. Children need to acquire the ability to take turns and this is usually done through play. Children take turns in many games and a child needs to be assertive enough to claim his share while not being so dominant as to take over completely. The child who does this is in danger of becoming a bully and will be avoided by others just as a child who is too reticent or timid will be ignored. The way a child's parents behave is crucial here. Those who listen to each other and make the time to talk and listen to their child provide an essential and gentle introduction to social skills.

So many of our everyday courtesies involve turn-taking; a child who learns to wait for a chance to talk to Grandma on the telephone, for instance, is learning how to hold back – never an easy lesson. A child who waits patiently must always be rewarded and get his turn or he will stop trying and may become aggressive or withdrawn. A child who learns about turn-taking at home will settle in more quickly in other social environments.

Allow her to take responsibility for some things

If a child is to feel responsible for her own actions she needs to feel she has some control over what she does and how she does it. Parents should encourage a child to take responsibility, but within reason. A child needs a realistic view of her powers and limitations and should not see these as weaknesses but as a fact of life. The limitations will decrease as she grows older. Parents who always interrupt what a child is doing to interfere or tell them what to do will produce a child who feels she has no control over her own actions and is therefore not responsible for them.

A child who is confident in her parents' love and goodwill is more likely to own up to a misdemeanour and apologize. Children should be encouraged to say they are sorry to each other if there is a mishap – for instance, if one knocks another over, she should apologize and see if she can do anything to make amends, such as pick up something that has been dropped, help clean up or whatever seems appropriate at the time. A child also needs to be able to receive an apology graciously – it is quite legitimate to say how hurt or upset she is but she should acknowledge an apology which is sincerely given.

Allow her to help you and others

Once again, if you want your child to be helpful and considerate she should see you being so. If you show that you care about other people and their feelings as a matter of course, your child will assimilate this. You can also take a more active role by discussing how other people feel and asking her to carry out a small task – for example, bringing in an elderly relative's book so they won't have to get up – because it will help to make someone else's life a bit easier.

Of course your expectations of how your child behaves must be in keeping with her age. Small children of three or so will often perform little tasks for others. They will want to please and enjoy being praised for their actions without consciously thinking how these actions affect other people. As a child gets to school age, she can take this on board and can be encouraged to do so. A child who behaves considerately and in a caring way tends to get positive feedback and this increases her self-esteem.

Help her to understand how others feel

By the age of seven most children are able to take other people's needs and feelings into account. They can sympathize with a child who has fallen over and hurt herself or who is not treated well at home, and they are also learning how to make moral judgements. By this age they have experience of a wider society, in school and clubs. They see that others do sometimes get away with naughty or unpleasant acts. They have a great sense of what is just – how often do you hear, 'It's not fair . . .'? This is confusing for the child and it helps to talk through situations, to discuss how you would act in certain circumstances and how these actions will have certain consequences. You can make a game of it and act out the roles.

If you are prepared to talk about things rather than issue orders, and to encourage children to weigh up the evidence, you will be giving your a child a great start in the moral maze!

Encourage modesty

Achievements should always be acknowledged and praised, but it isn't a good idea to let a child think she is some sort of genius. As a child struggles to conquer so many skills from tying a shoelace to studying for GCSEs, she needs to know that while she has had trouble with some skills she has found others easier and has done well or even extremely well; but a balance must be kept. If children have a real aptitude for something it's a good idea to encourage them to accept compliments with modesty. For instance, if they have been awarded lots of badges for swimming skills and are used as a comparison for other children in terms like 'Look at Judy, see how many badges she's got and she's younger than you!', you could teach Judy to reply that she's been going to swimming classes a long time and she also practises a lot. Children who constantly boast about how good they are at swimming or football or some other skill are seldom popular.

Show her how to win and lose

Playing board games is an excellent way of learning many social skills like taking turns, sharing, cooperating and negotiating. A parent may fall into the pitfall of always letting the child win, and if the child has no experience of losing she will find it difficult to come to terms with it when she plays with other children.

When a child is just learning a game or is quite young it's perfectly acceptable for them to be given some leeway in respect of the rules (for instance, playing Ludo can be hell if you haven't thrown a six in umpteen goes); however, an older child must learn to take the rough with the smooth. If you're playing a game which requires a certain amount of skill, like draughts or dominoes, it's quite a nice idea to explain your moves to a child so that she can learn the strategies, for it is demoralizing for a child to lose all the time to a parent. That is why it is so important for children to play games with other children, when they can compete on far more evenly matched terms.

A bone of contention that often arises between children is that each child follows a different set of rules. This has been known to happen even when playing snap! One way round this is to suggest to the children that they follow the rules which are used in your house and play by the other child's at his home; another is to have a compendium of rules handy, then if there's a dispute you can consult an independent source! Two excellent tomes produced by the Diagram Group and published by Collins are *Rules of the Game: Complete Encyclopaedia of all the Sports of the World* and *The Way To Play*, which covers indoor pastimes and games.

Children also have to learn to be both good winners and good losers. It's easy to smile when you win, but a child should be encouraged not to gloat over his victories just as a child who has lost a game shouldn't go off in a huff or sit and sulk (even though some adults still react to losing like this!). Children have to be taught that while some games require a lot of skill and practice, to win or lose at others is simply the luck of the draw.

I don't suppose there's a child in the world who has never cheated in a game – whether it be knocking the dice to produce another number, deliberately miscounting squares or glancing at another player's cards without them knowing. But children have to learn that cheats never prosper and cheats soon find that they are short of friends to play with. Generally as children become more skilled at games there is less tendency or need to cheat.

Help her cope with anger

Just as with other emotions, children have to learn to control their anger and to express it appropriately. They have to learn that it is quite normal and often justifiable to feel angry in certain situations and that we all have to learn strategies to deal with anger.

If you and your child are used to discussing how you feel, it should be easier for her to tell you she is feeling angry. Always ask *what* made you angry, not *who*; you don't want it to become personal, it serves no purpose. For example: 'I feel angry because my watch has been broken.' Anger needs a release; adrenalin builds up in the body needing a physical release. Some children might like to kick a ball against a wall, run very fast, put on some loud music and dance or if they're older they might like to try some relaxation techniques or strategies:

- learn to do a yoga complete breath
- learn the yoga alternate nostril breathing technique
- learn complete body relaxation
- listen to soothing music
- take a relaxing bath containing an aromatherapy oil
- have a massage

Demonstrate self-control

A child has to learn that it is sometimes necessary to moderate or control her own behaviour. There will be times when she will have to be willing to stop doing a favourite thing if necessary; for example when another child comes to play and refuses to play a certain game or is unwilling to try out the climbing frame in the garden. A child will learn valuable lessons in negotiation and in making someone feel welcome and at ease in her home. A child who has mastered this art will be quite willing to offer a favourite toy or belonging if required, and will soon learn to be sensitive to other children's needs. Children with siblings are often told to be nice to their sister or brother; a way to compensate for this with the only child is to offer examples like, 'Be nice to your friend Judy, she's just broken her favourite doll.'

A child who cries easily when she can't do something or goes into a sulk needs to be taught to fend for herself a little more and needs to learn to be more persistent and persevering. It is also essential for the child to begin to understand that it isn't important or appropriate for her to be able to do everything to perfection. Explain that trying to do something as best she can is what matters.

> ## Social skills you should aim for
> You know you're winning when your child:
>
> - is happy to do things for others when asked
> - likes to play games and perform tasks with other children
> - is modest and helps other children in group activity
> - actively joins in group activities and shares responsibility

Social games

Games that involve role playing are usually a great hit with younger children. What might seem rather humdrum to adults is huge fun for them and they are learning a great deal about social interacting. Children usually play these on their own initiative but sometimes they need a little prompting. It often helps if you play the game with your child if she is very timid and needs a bit of confidence-boosting. Try to think back to what you loved playing as a child and introduce your child to similar games, choosing a time when your child is receptive to a shared game (never force play on to a child, it becomes a chore and a duty for them for instance you might want to teach your child chess but if he isn't ready to learn or finds the whole process too tedious you'll defeat the object).

Most play-acting games require very few props and children are usually wonderfully creative here.

> ## A few hints for social games:
> Role playing puts children in everyday (usually adult) situations and allows them to work out the social codes, such as learning to queue and wait one's turn in a shop. Games also teach abstract concepts like trust and cooperation.
>
> - Mothers and fathers
> - Visiting friends
> - Playing shops: set up a table with a few everyday items and price them if your child can count, and so on
> - Set up a restaurant or café: with real or pretend food
> - Doctors or hospitals
> - Schools: let the child be the teacher

Listen to what your child says while she is playing, it can be most enlightening. You'll often hear your own voice and favourite phrases as well as those of other people in your child's life. Sometimes little problems which have been niggling a child surface and you can find a solution within the game which will give her ideas for how to solve things in real life. In fact the ability to be able to play as a child often determines a person's success in social activity later in life.

PARENT TRAPS

Don't:
- ignore an only child
- fail to notice when things are done
- always allow your child to win games
- always win games yourself
- fail to set limits

SUMMARY

Social skills don't just happen, they're acquired, and the more socially adept your child is the easier she will find her time at school. Only children may have a slight advantage in this area but as mentioned throughout this book it is the quality of parenting which counts. Teaching, by example, your child to be polite, helpful, modest and caring is an excellent preparation for life.

Chapter 6
Things your child may say and do

Whatever a family's situation in life, you can guarantee that children will ask awkward questions, usually at the most inconvenient moment. I can vividly remember standing in a crowded building society office one Saturday morning when my daughter asked in a loud, clear voice, 'Mummy, why haven't you got a husband?' Just about every head turned and there seemed to be a decided hush as everyone appeared to be waiting with bated breath for my answer.

We must realize that as adults we are endlessly fascinating to our children who know next to nothing about our existence before they came into the world. Once children are articulate enough to pose questions they begin to realize how little they know of their parents' past. I was once describing to my daughter my first experience of eating a curry which had been cooked by a boyfriend. The curry was forgotten – she immediately picked up the word 'boyfriend'. 'You had a boyfriend?' she asked incredulously. 'Did Nana know?' And just as a child is agog to know where they came from and how they got there, she also considers the possibility that others may follow her.

WHEN WILL I HAVE A BROTHER OR A SISTER?

It seems that every only child will ask about having a sibling at some stage or another, just as children who already have brothers and sisters may ask about having more – or sending back the ones they do have! Usually the question arises around the age of four or five, when they start school or nursery or when friends who are first-borns start acquiring baby brothers and sisters.

Some children, like Lucy, who has always told her mother she didn't want her mummy to have another baby, like the idea of babies when they see them in other people's houses and then think differently once they get home. Some will ask why they haven't got a brother or sister once or twice and then not bother any more; others will be more persistent. If your child is one of the persistent ones, just give the same reason each time. If you change the reason your child may think there's a crack in the defence and keep on and on at you. Eventually an answer that has been given consistently will be accepted. You could explain that deciding how many children to have is a decision adults make, like deciding where to live. Your child's age will determine how you respond to the question.

Obviously, when she's very young, long, complicated explanations about keeping the world's population in check will mean nothing to her: a simple statement like 'We only ever wanted one child and you're so lovely . . .' is usually quite acceptable.

Health reasons can be simplified so that even a young child can accept them. Something along the lines of, 'Mummy was very ill after I had you and I didn't want to be ill again when you needed me to look after you,' is usually accepted quite readily.

Children generally worry about age, growing old and dying so I personally wouldn't offer the fact that you were an older mother as a reason. Saying, 'Oh, I'm too old to have any more,' might have the child worrying unnecessarily about your imminent demise!

Whatever your own reasons, stick closely to the truth if you can. Saying something like the stork only delivered one, or perhaps the stork got lost with the second baby, will only store problems for you later and you could find that you've painted yourself into the proverbial corner.

Sometimes, however, it isn't kind to be too truthful. For instance, if your pregnancy was so difficult that it put you off having any more children, it might not be appropriate to tell your child this. It could place an inordinate amount of blame on to the child, who will feel, whether consciously or not, guilty at having made you suffer so much. Similarly, if the first months of your child's life were a horrendous ordeal, when she cried from morning to night and wore you out so much that you decided *never again*, it might be wiser to save the confession until the child is much older.

It has been suggested in some studies that if the mother shows no interest in having another baby, her child will react similarly. The main thing for parents to remember is to be as honest as possible, at the same time as being as positive as you can about the fact that your child is an only – after all, there are obvious advantages which you can explain to your child. Above all, do not allow yourself to be made to feel guilty. Whatever your reasons for not having any more children, they were probably good ones.

For a child living with one parent, the question of siblings can be just as pressing, and even when you think you've got a foolproof answer it isn't always so – as one mother found out.

When Chrissie asked me why she couldn't have a baby brother or sister I replied that it wasn't possible as we didn't have a daddy living with us. At first she thought her father, my ex-partner, would supply another baby and when I explained that that was impossible as we didn't see him any more she looked thoughtful then said, 'Well, I'm sure somebody will help you out.' I suddenly had this vision of her approaching men in the street asking them to give her mother a baby!

This is another side of single parenting that rather surprised and shocked Sara, mother of eight-year-old Edwin.

Edwin told me how much he liked his swimming teacher and I said something like, 'Yes, he's very nice, isn't he?' Only to have my son reply, 'I'd like him to be my daddy and then I could have a brother.'

Parents should always try to be very positive about having an only child, saying how delighted you are with her, perhaps. Be reassured that having no siblings will not blight a child's life and if he wasn't asking about a brother he'd probably be after something else. It's a fact of life that children will always ask for something they can't have, like a new computer that is beyond your means or a large dog when you live in a flat. No one gets everything they want in life and that's something we all have to learn.

One thing you should not do is to try and compensate a child for being an only by buying her things – that will only serve to confirm in her mind that she is indeed missing out by not having siblings. An only child needs no more toys than a child with siblings. In addition if she is receiving extra presents to make her feel special, it may distance her from her friends who do not have all the extras.

MUMMY, I'M LONELY

I once asked Olivia if she was ever lonely and she replied that no, she wasn't and when I wasn't around she had her dolls to keep her company. I took this to mean when I wasn't in the same room as her. At seven, she has never mentioned loneliness to me but I dare say that day may come. As we get older we realize that we can be lonely in a crowd of people, within a relationship or a family, and not feel lonely when we are actually alone.

However, children do play the 'I'm bored and lonely' card when they're trying to persuade you to provide siblings. One mother, Sue, has always known that she was only going to have one child and does all the right things to give her son, Tom, an interesting and stimulating life. Recently he has been seeing a lot of two sets of cousins, both boys; witnessing their relationships, he thinks he is missing out and is forever telling his parents he is 'bored and lonely'. It doesn't help much to know it's only a stage he's going through. The problem is – and this happens frequently – that siblings react better to one another and play together more companionably when there is an outside influence. Thus Tom, playing with his cousins, sees them at their best and not when they are squabbling and and niggling with each other, or competing for parental attention.

It's a difficult situation, but you can't magic siblings out of the air. All you can do is emphasize the positive aspects of being an only, point out the disadvantages of having siblings (for your family) and offer plenty of company, both yours and other children's.

Young children often offer 'I'm lonely in bed on my own' as an excuse to get in bed with you or join you in the sitting-room after their bedtime. Most children go through this stage and it doesn't just apply to only children. The corollary to this is that in families where there are more children one child will use another as an excuse to leave his bed, saying things like: 'Nadia's light/breathing/radio/snoring is keeping me awake.'

However the 'I'm lonely' tactic used by a child must never be confused with the very real problem loneliness can be for some children. It's one that you might have overlooked or not been aware of. When a child says 'I'm lonely at school/in the playground/in my class/at the after-school club,' this statement should be investigated; it may be a one-off feeling because her best friend wasn't there that day or she was feeling out of sorts with the world but it could be a situation that has developed and needs to be resolved (see Chapters Four and Five for detailed strategies and advice). One thing that you can be sure of is that being an only child is not a prerequisite to being a lonely one.

MUMMY, I'M BORED

In the National Child Development Study analysed by Ann Laybourn, which compared the only child with a one-sibling child, 66 per cent of eleven-year-old onlies said they were bored sometimes or often compared with 75 per cent of children with a brother or sister. This would imply that only children are better at entertaining themselves. Inevitably some children will bore more readily than others, but a child who's used to varied and comprehensive activities is less likely to feel that life is tedious.

A young child is unlikely to articulate his boredom but will display his feelings by his actions. Toys that no longer engage his attention will be discarded, kicked or ignored, and it's up to the adult to suggest a change of game or activity. Once children are at school, and sometimes before, they acquire the word 'boring' and seem to use it to maximum effect usually to irritate a parent.

While they are still quite young, children may need an adult to supervise or help them with some activities like cooking, wood-work, sewing, knitting or origami, either because of the possible danger or because small hands are not so dexterous and need direction. Preventing your child from being bored need not involve expensive toys or apparatus. Most children like making things from junk materials found around the home: cereal and egg boxes, pieces of fabric, straws, etc. It's a good idea to keep a small supply handy so you don't have to waste time and tempers on trying to find what you require when you actually need it.

A child who feels she has some control over her environment and what she does will be able to amuse herself more readily especially if she has access to materials for crafts and creative play. You can allow your child a greater feeling of independence and yourself some space and time if you lay a few ground rules:

- establish one area as a designated place to work at – like the kitchen table and not the coffee table in the sitting-room
- leave an apron and some sort of protection for the table, if this is necessary, to hand
- have scissors (appropriate to the child's age), glue and paint in a place which can be easily reached

With the minimum amount of forward planning and organization, your child can go off and be creative without having to worry you each time. All you have to do is offer assistance if required and check progress from time to time.

Often a child will feel bored when she is making a transition from one stage of development to another. The jigsaw puzzles and games she has are too easy now, or she's moved on from dolls and isn't quite sure what she wants to do. So if your child constantly complains of being bored, check to see if the activities she has match or stretch his capabilities. If not, introduce some new ones. Car boot sales are always a good source of hardly used toys at reasonable prices. If your child receives a mountain of gifts at Christmas and birthdays, try to arrange for some which will come into their own when she is, say, six months older and then put them away somewhere. That way you'll always have something new and exciting to offer.

An only child is less likely to say she is bored than a child who has a sibling as we have seen from the survey. However you will have to fill the role in playing board and card games that require more than one player if she doesn't have a friend round to play. As she gets older you can introduce games of solitaire, and if chess is one of her games, a computerized chess board that supplies the opponent may be a worthwhile investment.

Although television has its uses and usefulness, don't be tempted into making it your babysitter. Younger children may need someone with them while they are watching a programme, to explain things and to make sure that what they are watching is appropriate to their age. Older children, especially pubescent ones, will often take root in front of a screen and should be encouraged into other activities, in particular those involving some physical exertion. It's fine to flop down in front of the TV after a hectic and active day, but not to spend the whole day in front of the box in a state of inertia, as the now proverbial couch potato.

MY MUMMY'S HAVING A BABY

Children have always had vivid imaginations and like to talk about things they would wish to happen as though they really are about to. Just as a child will announce to his friends that he's going to Disneyland (before consulting his parents, who may have no intention of making such a trip) so children will say that their mother is pregnant. Single children are not the only ones who like to imagine that their mother is having another baby. My own mother was congratulated on her forthcoming happy event by my younger sister's class teacher. Apparently it had been a much-discussed item in her news book.

Parents shouldn't overact and accuse the child of deliberately making things up or lying. The younger the child the more blurred the boundaries between what is real and what they would like to be real, and you never know she might have overheard something that gave her the wrong impression. There is also an element of competition and conformity among children here. One child will boast that her mummy is having a baby and before you know it half the neighbourhood is in a similar state, every other child having declared solidarity.

If you have made a firm commitment to having one child, you can tell this to your offspring. Don't be tempted to say things like 'maybe one day . . .' or you'll be pestered to name the day for ever after.

FANTASY SIBLINGS

Only children often fantasize about having a brother or a sister or siblings in the plural. For some children they become just like imaginary friends and unseen companions. For others a fantasy brother or sister is just someone they refer to in vague terms often when they need a collaborator or an excuse to have something she wants. Olivia has always wanted bunk beds and so has come up with the solution: 'If I had a sister we could have bunk beds and I could sleep on the top . . .'

In general terms an only child's fantasies are totally unrealistic. Olivia's fantasy sister, who by the way has only made one or two appearances, would not argue with her about who should have the top bunk. The fantasy sister does not have a mind of her own and certainly is not seen as someone who will borrow something and then forget to put it away so it ends up getting broken. The fantasy brother will be a paragon, someone who will never tease her for being a girl, as real brothers are apt to.

IMAGINARY FRIENDS

I wonder how many adults can remember their own imaginary friends? I can vaguely remember mine and I also remember what my own parents told me of him (contrary to the usual pattern, mine was not the same sex as me). My friend was the doctor. I think he probably arrived at about the same time as my sister was born, when I was two and a half and he had left by the time we moved house when I was five. My parents would often come into a room and be told not to sit in a certain seat as the doctor was sitting there. My own daughter has not had an imaginary friend –

maybe because she's had enough real ones – but she certainly has anthropomorphized her toy animals and dolls and they often get the blame for the untidiness in her room!

Imaginary playmates are a normal part of growing up for some children. They usually come into existence when the child is between the ages of three and six and they are not exclusive to only children, so there's no need to worry that your child is feeling isolated or lonely if he has invented a chum to play with. For the child these fantasy playmates are real and quite often they will make room for him in bed or at the dinner table. Some children turn to their friend for comfort or commiseration when they have been told off for some misdemeanour or as a confidant with whom they can share their secrets, while others use the invisible child as a scapegoat – one friend's child calls his Tommy Trouble. If anything has gone wrong, been broken or damaged your child will rather conveniently blame his imaginary friend.

Generally a fantasy friend is used to make games more exciting and only if the fantasy remains central to your child's games for a long period should you consider the possibility that he needs more opportunity to play with other children of his own age. Usually a fantasy friend is used to practise his social skills so that he is more adept at them in real life. Although some children hang on to their little playmates for longer and take time to give them up completely, most fantasy friends tend to vanish into thin air by the time a child has started school.

HELPING YOUR CHILD TO FEEL GOOD ABOUT BEING AN ONLY

The chances are that with more and more people choosing to limit their families your only child has at least one friend who is also without siblings and that you also have friends or family who have one child. It is good for your child to mix with other onlies to see that it is quite a normal and acceptable state of affairs.

Equally it is important for your child to witness what life is like in larger families. Overnight stays with another family can be quite revealing and only children soon learn that brothers and sisters are just as likely to fight and squabble as they are to play together.

If you know someone who has a baby it would be helpful if your child could spend some time with them, helping to look after the baby if that is appropriate to your child's age. My own daughter adores visiting friends with babies and is becoming quite an expert at holding and entertaining them. You could also invite a younger child to stay overnight with you so that yours could witness the realities of having someone younger around the house (but do put away any particularly loved possession of your child that could end up broken!).

Best of all try to make sure you spend time with your child and that she is enjoying life with lots of friends and keeping in touch with your extended family (see Chapter Eleven).

When discussing your child's status as an only, I don't think it's helpful to say one type of family is better than another. If you've told your child that a lot of children in a family means they often don't get enough attention, imagine the scene when you visit one such family and your own offspring pipes up that children in large families get neglected! As stated earlier, families come in all shapes and sizes and each has its advantages. What we have to work out as individuals is what is right for us and stick by our guns when criticized for having an only.

PARENT TRAPS

Too much sophistication
The only child does have a unique advantage in that she has access to adult company that doesn't have to be shared with another child. If the parent isn't careful the child can become too old for her years. Rather like the Victorians who dressed their children as mini-adults, so today's parents may make the only child too sophisticated, so that she becomes distanced from her peer group. Then she will find it more difficult to socialize as she has less in common. This is particularly true of younger children.

One way round this is to try to maintain a balance in your child's activities. If you've introduced your child to the ballet and she loves it, that's fine. But if none of her friends go, it's more difficult to share and talk about her experiences. You could, of course, ask her to invite a friend next time; but you can also make sure she sees the latest Disney or whatever film is currently in vogue, so that she won't feel left out when all her classmates talk about it in the playground.

Too much babying

One problem of having just one child is that as she grows out of babyhood another doesn't take her place, and there may be a temptation for some parents to continue 'babying' a child when this is inappropriate. The growing-up process entails the baby growing into childhood, seeing itself as a separate being. If this does not happen, the child will display behaviour that does not match his age and which he may find embarrassing as he attends playgroup, nursery or school.

Not seeing imaginary friends

As discussed above imaginary friends and fantasy siblings are a normal part of growing up for many children and they get a great deal of satisfaction from them. Your child will feel upset and confused if you refuse to 'see' them or acknowledge their existence. So join in the game just as you would when your child is playing with dolls or toy soldiers and has created a whole make-believe world.

Painting yourself into a corner

Parents always have to be alert to what they are saying to their child and the messages that may be implied in their words. As I have suggested above, as far as possible and within reason honesty is always a good policy when dealing with awkward questions. What you don't want to do is paint yourself into a corner by promising something that you simply won't be able to deliver. An example of this is to say, 'We would have another child if we could afford it.' A child who decides he would very much like a brother or sister might then become involved in all sorts of money-making schemes, having no idea of the real costs involved. Or may pester you with, 'Well, could we have another baby if you won the lottery, the football pools', or such and such a competition. For everyone's peace of mind, a child needs to know and understand what is a distinct possibility and what is extremely unlikely or impossible.

SUMMARY

Only children often ask why they don't have a sibling or if you could arrange one. Whatever your response, be consistent and in time the child will accept the status quo. What any child needs is to be loved and wanted regardless of the number or lack of siblings.

Chapter 7

Encouraging independence

T HE ULTIMATE goal in child rearing is to bring up another human being who can live independently of you. At the beginning of life the child is totally dependent on you for everything but eventually she will have to learn to do everything for herself. Emotionally, too, she will have to move away from you and the successful parents will bring up a child able to leave the family 'nest' and create her own with a whole network of new relationships. Within a healthy family, the bond will still be strong with members offering each other support when needed. In an unhealthy family a child will be unable to make the break and the parents will still control and manipulate.

THE ROAD TO INDEPENDENCE

Achieving independence is a gradual thing, it's not something you acquire suddenly at a certain age like the key to the door. There are steps along the way and the competent parent will make sure there is a natural progression from one to the next. However, that does not mean that we as parents will all follow the same path. Some parents will think that it is important to allow a child to cross a road on her own and go into a shop to buy something by a certain age. Others with a child of the same age might be horrified at the thought, but are quite happy for their child to make a cup of tea or coffee and carry it to another room.

My daughter first brought me breakfast in bed (no coffee, though!) on my birthday when she was about four, and I have planned my kitchen cupboards so that she can reach the plates, cups and bowls she needs without standing on a chair, if she wants to help herself to something to eat. She now feels quite confident using the kettle and makes a decent cup of coffee. Much against my own judgement, as she kept pestering me I have let her use the iron. She did burn her finger slightly once but I think that has made her more careful now. She was right, she knew she was ready to tackle the new task. Sometimes we may be unwittingly holding our child back from acquiring skills they are ready for.

ACTING INDEPENDENTLY

It's worth making a list every now and again to assess how your child is progressing, and we should remember that no one acquires skills overnight. You can't always go from you doing the thing for her to the child doing the job competently on her own. Life is like learning to read: first the adult reads to the child, then they read together, the child then reads some words by herself with you still there to prompt him, until he gradually takes over and has mastered the skill. So as our child gets older we must explain what we are doing while we are doing it. It's no good sitting a child in a bath and assuming he has washed himself, he has to know what to do and why it is important.

Between the ages of five and eleven children make massive leaps in what they can do without you and there are situations where you will have to teach them what to do even though they will not be doing it on their own for some time. For example, learning to cross the road safely is something you should instil in your child as early as possible, even though she won't be on her own for some time. Some children are very good near roads, others have absolutely no sense of the inherent danger, it's something he should pick up at an early age – and as with other skills he will follow your lead, so it's no good showing him what to do when he's eventually on his own, only to dash across the road, dodging cars with scarcely a thought to safety while your child clings on to your hand.

Activities checklist

Here are some activities that your child will have to do for himself at some time. Think about where he's at now. Are you currently teaching him, does he do it now without supervision or is it an activity which you will start teaching in the future? If the last one is the case, think about at what age you will start and consider that you might need to reassess your time scale and bring things forward.

- bathing alone
- cleaning his teeth unsupervised
- washing his hair
- selecting what to wear
- styling his hair
- cutting his nails
- tidying up
- dusting
- using the vacuum cleaner
- ironing
- laying the table
- washing up or loading the dishwasher
- making coffee and tea
- using the microwave oven
- washing clothes
- crossing the road
- going out to post a letter
- going to a local shop
- being responsible for a pet
- using a telephone at home and in a public call-box

Many of these activities the child will learn as he helps you out in the home. Only turn down offers to help if you are in a real rush, otherwise allow more time. Be careful to explain what you want done, don't assume the child knows automatically because he's seen you do it a thousand times. Always encourage and point out the things the child did well. If there is a disaster, don't over-react and be sympathetic.

Going to school alone

One advantage of having a younger sibling is that a parent can take them both to school without the older one losing face in front of her friends. When the newspapers and media are full of horror stories of children being abducted or killed it is easy to lose sight of the fact that that this is still a relatively rare occurrence. When a child is at a local school within walking distance, parents may begin to give more independence progressively by leaving her at the school gate, not going into the playground; seeing her across a major road and then letting her go on alone; allowing her to go with an older friend; seeing her off with friends in her own year.

Being alone in the house

Individual parents have to decide when they feel the time is right for a child to be left alone in the house. The law is non-specific here. While leaving a child alone is not an offence in itself, if the child suffers in any way because she was on her own the parent could then be charged with neglect. Parents have a duty to see that their children, and any others who may be visiting, will come to no harm in the home.

By the time a child has reached the age of nine or ten many parents allow them to be in home alone after school, or with one or two school friends. But from whatever age, your child should be aware of personal safety and what to do in emergencies.

Answering the phone

From a safety point of view, children should be taught how to answer the phone in a way which will protect them from nuisance callers and people who have an unnatural interest in children.

- Always answer the phone with 'hello', never give the number
- If the child doesn't recognize the voice, she should ask who the caller wants to speak to
- If a parent isn't in the house for whatever reason, the child should say that Mummy or Daddy isn't available at the moment, can he or she call back later or can the child take a message

- If the caller is persistent and asks where the parent is, the child should reply that he or she is in the bath
- Teach your child to know that she doesn't have to answer questions on the phone and if anyone should say anything unpleasant to her she should hang up immediately

Answering the door

Young children should never answer the door unless they know who is there (by checking through a window or spyhole). If you have a chain on the door you can train your child to use it if she really needs to open the door. By the time a child is coming home from school on her own, and may be in the house for an hour or so before a parent gets home, it is wiser if they make it a rule never to answer the door to strangers. Anyone who really needs to see you will come back.

Emergencies

A child should know from an early age that you can ring 999 in cases of fire or accident. Many children have saved a parent's life by dialling for help! Your child should always have a number where he can contact you (if this is a work number give him your extension number and perhaps that of a colleague so if you are in a meeting or whatever you will be contacted in an emergency), and a list of numbers of your close friends who would know what to do and would be prepared to act in an emergency.

One practical idea is for the child to have a phone card or telephone charge card so that he can always call you if he needs to. It saves having to worry about having the right change for the phone and a charge-card type means he can ask to make a call from anywhere and the charge will be billed to you. Your child should also be aware how to make a reversed charges call.

Respecting your child's privacy

I think parents should always respect a child's privacy and starting this early means it becomes a way of life not something you have to begin as your child enters adolescence. Things like not walking into a bathroom when she is using the shower, knocking on bedroom doors, not opening letters addressed to the child, not reading diaries and so on should all follow as a matter of course. If you expect a child to respect your own need for privacy, show her the same consideration.

THE ADOLESCENT ONLY

Children need to learn how to be an adult and do adult things within a controlled setting, and that is usually the home. For instance, you might be against gambling as an activity, but children need to learn that the excitement of winning is balanced by the despondency of losing. Playing games which involve betting and using pennies is a way of illustrating this without involving your children in casinos or turf accountants!

Equally as you child gets older you might want to allow him to sample alcohol. A sixteen-year-old can legally have a glass of wine with a meal in a restaurant, so why not at home? French families begin by offering their children watered down wine. You need to explain the dangers of drinking too much alcohol – the way it adversely affects your body and your mind – and lead by example.

As children grow into teenagers there are the inevitable disputes over what is allowed, times to be home by, fashion, personal hygiene whatever. It is worth bearing in mind if you are laying down the law about something that your offspring will be allowed to do most things whether you like it or not within a very short space of time.

At thirteen your child is legally able to:

- take on a part-time job – although this must not be during the school day or before seven in the morning or after seven in the evening and must not exceed two hours on a Sunday or school day.

At sixteen your child will be legally entitled to:

- leave school
- take up full-time work (within local authority restrictions)
- marry with parental consent or apply for a court authorization
- apply for a passport with the consent of one parent
- consent to sexual intercourse (girls)

- hold a moped licence
- buy cigarettes
- drink alcohol with a meal in a restaurant
- buy fireworks
- buy Premium Bonds
- join a trade union
- join the armed forces (boys)
- consent to or refuse medical, surgical or dental treatment
- buy a lottery ticket

An eighteen-year-old is to all intents and purposes an adult with very few restrictions. This is the age of majority and among other things your child can:

- vote
- marry without your consent
- drink alcohol in licensed premises
- be called upon for jury service
- change her name without your consent
- apply for a passport without your consent
- open a bank account in her own right
- consenting to a homosexual relationship (men)

However there are still a few things your child has to wait until she or he is twenty-one for, and these are:

- seeking election as a local councillor or MP
- having a licence to sell alcohol
- adopting a child

Allowing your child the freedom to run risks

If you're constantly worried about losing your child or something awful happening to him and so restrict his movements, you will make him resentful (and perhaps deceitful as he will go off and do things with or without your consent and may lie to cover his tracks). You can't live life for your child and nor can you prevent him from taking risks or making mistakes. You can obviously guide him and point out pitfalls but in the end he has to make his own decisions. You must be there for him if things go wrong and he needs a shoulder to cry on or other support.

Relaxing and not being overly anxious

This is a difficult one. Some parents are naturally relaxed in their parenting, others just can't help being anxious all the time, often with little reason. However, while it may be natural to feel anxious about some things (first time away from home, first day in a new school), you can't worry every time your son leaves the house that he might get run over by a car.

Try and minimize what you are anxious about. For instance if you have instilled in your child the importance of telling you where he is and what time he will be returning by, it's pointless to start worrying that he isn't back half an hour before he is due.

If you always know where your child is, who he is with, vaguely what they are planning to do and when he will be back, then you should be less anxious. Anxiety is often provoked by not knowing something.

House rules for guests

As mentioned in Chapter Eleven, most households have an unwritten code that they practice. When your child gets older and may be in the home at some time on his own, he should be aware of your edicts and follow them. For instance, if you've experienced coming home to a bomb site and finding every scrap of food gone from the fridge, you might impose a 'no friends while we're out' rule, or limit the number to one or two who won't leave the place looking like a war zone.

Yvonne encourages her sixteen-year-old son Dorian to bring his friends home but she was furious when one walked dog mess through her house and upstairs to the bathroom. 'I couldn't believe it! My bathroom carpet was ruined and I had to throw it out. I made Dorian clean the stair carpet and told him his friends better wipe his feet next time or else!' And they will, mainly because they like going round to Dorian's home as his mum will often cook them a meal, and there's an enormous range of video films which Yvonne collects.

Whatever the rules are in your home, and the fewer and simpler they are the better, make sure your child is properly aware of them and that they equally apply to guests.

LEAVING HOME

My mum's on her own – she left my father because she thought his mental illness was having an adverse effect on me. Although she worked full-time I was the centre of her attention. I always felt sorry for her situation and I saw how hard it was for her bringing up a daughter on her own. She always spoke to me as a friend and I never felt the need to rebel as other teenagers did. She would always listen to what I had to say. However, I had the feeling that I had to get away. She's lovely but quite dominating. As I've got older people have asked me, 'Don't you feel bad about leaving your mum on her own?' but I don't.

At some stage in his life your child will leave home and this is something you just have to be prepared for. I don't think it's any harder for parents of onlies than it is for parents of larger families. Each departure is a wrench. Some couples look forward to having the house to themselves again, others dread an emptiness the child will leave behind. How you feel depends very much on the life you've lived. If you've brought your child up to be confident in his own abilities the chances are, after the initial shock, you'll confidently get on with your own life too.

Maintaining your own social life and relationships

This is important whatever the age of your child, as has been mentioned in earlier chapters. However, once your child reaches secondary school and begins to have a more independent social life it is imperative for you to maintain yours. If you have tended not to socialize much when your child was younger you may need to jump-start your own social activities. Here are some ideas:

- join the local film society
- join a sports or leisure club
- enrol for an evening course in something that's always appealed to you
- renew old acquaintances
- have a party and invite all your old friends, that way you should receive some return invitations

PARENT TRAPS

Becoming a burden to your child

Perhaps no one sets out to deliberately burden their offspring – although one does wonder, when you hear what some families get up to to keep the children with them – but it does happen. A child can be weighed down by the problems of the parent or with the parent. You should never assume that a child will look after you in old age or sickness, unless he wants to. What you have to do is plan your own life taking things like illness and and old age into consideration.

Making the child feel guilty

As with most of the parent traps I have described which could equally well apply to parents of more than one child, making a child feel guilty falls into this category. Some parents have made this into an art form, and with just a certain look or a sigh can make a child feel totally unreasonable for wanting to go out and leave them for whatever reason. Equally, a child shouldn't be made to feel responsible for things that have gone wrong in your life or haven't happened the way you might have liked them to, such as blaming a child for having to give up your career. That was your choice.

Making the child feel too precious

This has been discussed in previous chapters but it must be stressed that a child who is made to feel that she is someone exceptionally special will have troubles in making and sustaining relationships when two people need to be equal. This child would see a marriage of two people who are on the same footing as a demotion from the centre-stage and the spotlight.

SUMMARY

The moment a baby is born she sets off on the road towards independence from her parents. Most young children start off with a strong sense of independence – how often have you heard 'I can do that!'? – and it needs to be nurtured and encouraged throughout childhood, with tasks and skills acquired appropriate to age and ability. After all the very aim of parenthood is to provide the next generation with confident, capable adults.

Chapter 8

Promoting self-esteem

M<small>ANY PEOPLE</small> reach adulthood dissatisfied with their appearance, lacking confidence in their abilities and thinking they have no right to be successful or loved. They are severely disadvantaged by feelings of inadequacy and insecurity. Yet no baby is born with such low self-esteem. So what goes wrong?

Basically, insensitive or poor parenting produces children who grow up with little sense of their own worth. Often parents are unaware of how their actions and words are misinterpreted and they frequently suffer from poor self-esteem themselves.

How we learn to see and think of ourselves is based on how others have treated us and what they have told us about ourselves. This process begins from the moment of birth. How a baby is shown love or lack of it in the way she is handled, comforted, fed, spoken to, stroked all contribute to how she feels about herself.

Children brought up in institutions where their physical needs (home, food, clothing) are met most frequently suffer low self-esteem because their emotional needs have not been catered for. They feel abandoned and unloved and therefore in their own eyes must be unlovable. That is one end of a spectrum of care but even children raised in what on the surface seem to be loving and adequate families can experience a low self-worth, as we will see.

Initially the greatest influence on how a child feels about herself is her parents and family. The first ideas she has about herself are learned within the family. She hears herself described in certain ways and these labels help form her idea of who she is. Thus a child who hears positive comments will see herself in a positive light while those who hear more negative judgements will begin to think negatively about themselves. A child who is constantly called *stupid*, *clumsy*, *ugly*, *dumb* by parents whom she is biologically programmed to want to impress and seek approval from will think of herself in those terms. To her the adult must be right.

However, the way a child perceives herself is not just prompted by verbal clues. Parents can undermine their child's self-esteem and make her feel anxious about herself in a variety of ways. These include:

- dominating her
- treating her with indifference
- not respecting her
- making disparaging comments
- showing no admiration for what she has achieved
- being cold towards her
- isolating her
- discriminating against her

Few parents set out to reduce a child's self-esteem but, it must be said, some adults enjoy the power they have over children, especially if they perhaps have little influence in other areas of their lives. Other parents are afraid of showing too much approval, as Jenny reveals.

I was brought up in a very loving home but I never thought they were really proud of me. Whenever I did well at school or in some hobby their congratulations always seemed muted and I always felt I should somehow have done better. When I asked them about this, as an adult, they were literally flabbergasted. They told me they'd always been immensely proud of me but were afraid of spoiling me, making me too bigheaded, and were wary of seeming so themselves in front of neighbours and friends.

Some parents may in fact be jealous of their own offspring, and so become extra-critical and downplay the child's achievements.

There have been no studies which assess any differences in the self-esteem in only children compared with those who have siblings. One might feel that an only child – not having to compete for attention or put up with sibling rivalry and some of the consequent negative influences – would fare better, but that is not necessarily so. The important factor is not your family size but how your family interacts and sees itself, as Anna, an only now in her late thirties, comments:

> *My mother constantly undermined me. She always blamed me for the things that went wrong in her life. She never acknowledged any achievements and always played them down. I remember passing the eleven plus and she told me that I still wasn't going to as good a school as my cousins. She made me feel bad about myself and I lacked the confidence to do what I really wanted to do – go to university. In fact I did go but not straight from school. It took me years to build up my own sense of worth. I've done well, have my own home and run my own business, but she still tries to wrong-foot me, usually by trying to get me to agree to things that she knows will make things awkward for me and then moan about whatever we're doing afterwards.*

Whatever signals a young child is given, by the age of six or seven she is able to compare herself with the idea of who she would like to be. As she makes this comparison she sees how well she is faring in terms of her own expectations and those of others, like her parents and teachers, and begins to build up a sense of self-esteem.

For a child to have a sense of her own worth and be confident, she needs to feel that she is

- valued
- loved
- approved of by family and teachers
- capable of doing some things well, and that what she does well is appreciated
- basically good
- able to influence and control her life

A child who has high self-esteem tends to be popular in her group. Children with low self-esteem sometimes turn into bullies or become victims of bullying (see Chapter Four). To encourage high self-esteem in a child the parents need to be emotionally warm people who make strong but realistic demands for high standards in work and behaviour, and *realistic* is the operative word here. There is absolutely no point in setting standards that are way above your child's capabilities. That will just lead to guilt for the child when she doesn't live up to your demands, and a consequent loss of self-esteem.

A child may also feel guilty about her very existence. So if there are problems within the family, it's imperative that the child is made to realize that she is not responsible. If a parent loses a job, or a member of the family suffers an illness, or the parents separate or divorce or continually argue, the child may assume she is the root cause, especially if she has overheard conversations which were not intended for her ears. A child should be constantly reassured that she is loved and that sometimes adults have problems which make them angry or hurt but that neither these feelings nor the problems are caused by the child.

Lack of financial security can have a disruptive effect within a family and a child may assume she is a burden if there is no time or money to devote to her. A parent may unwittingly make the child feel guilty for outgrowing a pair of shoes when money is tight or for eating so much or wasting food when the household budget is limited. However, it does not follow that low-income families produce children who have low self-esteem – far from it. The crucial factor is the quality of the parent–child relationship. So, for example, a parent who doesn't work may not have a vast disposable income with which to buy treats and pay for expensive outings but does have the time to cherish a child, concentrate on her needs, organize low-cost entertainment and give her a brilliant start in life.

Parents who work hard and are ambitious for themselves often, paradoxically, undermine their child's self-esteem by being over critical and expecting their child to get perfect grades in school while failing to register the loneliness and isolation that child may feel as a result of parents who have so little time for her because of their own careers.

FEELING LOVED AND LOVABLE

This is a basic human need. A child must know she is loved unconditionally through word and action. Children are able to sense unspoken judgements (you may betray criticism by your body language and expressions that need no words to explain them) and they internalize them and therefore see themselves as failures, disappointments, inadequate or unloved.

When a child does something naughty or wrong it is the deed that should always be criticized, not the child, and it should be explained that that behaviour doesn't make the parent love the child any less. Although I always say this to my daughter, she often retorts that I couldn't possibly love her if she's naughty. I was delighted when the message seemed to have got through when I saw the Mother's Day card she'd made at school. I wasn't too happy with the word 'bad' until I realized it was easier to spell than most alternatives!

> *My mum*
> *My mum loves me*
> *My mum kisses me good night*
> *My mum takes me on outings*
> *My mum lets me go on her computer*
> *But best of all when I'm bad she still loves me*
>
> by Olivia, March 1996

When a parent's love is conditional on her performing in a certain way, the child soon learns to accept that any unacceptable behaviour or failure makes her unlovable and bad. Success, in that child's eyes, equals being good and loved. She learns that her worth is determined by other people and that this can fluctuate. Therefore she is never quite sure where she stands and her confidence will suffer as a result.

On the other hand a child who enjoys unconditional love will learn to accept criticism and failure rather than be devastated by it. She is convinced of her own worth and significance. She will feel competent and will learn that she has control over her own behaviour. She will have a strong sense of self and a belief that she can make things happen.

To achieve this, we as parents need to believe in a child's abilities and have confidence in her if she says she can do something. It is very tempting as well as understandable to want to protect a child from disappointment but if a child says she can do something and you reply something along the lines of 'Do you think you're ready for that yet . . . are you really sure you can . . . shouldn't you wait until . . .?' you will undermine her confidence. Far better to say, 'I expect you can, go on . . .' and be ready to praise her when she does it or commiserate if she doesn't but never in a 'told you so' kind of way. If you don't constantly underestimate your child, she won't grow up to undervalue herself. Over-protection and setting too many limits on her freedom to do things will also lead to a lack of self-esteem. This applies equally to parents of more than one child as to parents of only children. As parents we need to provide an opportunity for our child to test her competence at a whole range of activities that are appropriate to her age and development.

Not setting limits is equally detrimental to a child. If she is trying to do things without parental guidance, and too soon, this will lead to failure and her self-esteem will be diminished.

Children who demonstrate high self-esteem tend to have more boundaries. However, these are set with a certain amount of participation by the child (depending on her age) in deciding what the limits are and at what levels they should be set. An example is being able to do things on her own. A parent may agree that a child can now make a cup of coffee on her own but discussing the pitfalls they both agree that the child should not try to carry it up two flights of stairs. If the child receives an acknowledgement of her skills and is involved in deciding how to exercise them her confidence will be boosted. Constructive arguments can foster a child's sense of self-worth. Any disagreement is discussed and a child is allowed her viewpoint, which may at times override that of a parent. In this way we give our child a sense of power to affect or change things.

When a child does try out something new or more difficult, the outcome of the exercise should not be emphasized as more important than the process of learning about her abilities. It is imperative for the adult to interpret the child's experience in a positive way. For example, if your child is taking a 400-metre swimming badge but only manages 300 metres, praise her for this and encourage her with the fact that now she knows she can swim 300 metres she can work towards the 400 benchmark.

Throughout a person's lifetime levels of self-esteem can vary – we all receive blows to our morale from time to time and feel negatively about ourselves: an adult who was given a solid foundation in self-worth as a child finds it much easier to bounce back.

We should aim to give a child:

- a sense of her own significance: a child needs to know that she matters and that she is important in her own right, that she has her parent/carer's unconditional love and support
- a sense of competence: she needs to believe that she has control over her own behaviour, that she is good at some things and that she can master her environment
- a sense of being connected to others: no one likes to feel alienated and cut off from others, and we flourish when we feel part of a greater family, community, society, nation but this needs to be balanced by
- a sense of separate identity: she needs to feel that she is distinct from others, that she is an individual and is significant as such
- a sense of realism about herself and the world: this means the child should become aware that no one is perfect but that adults can offer constructive advice on how to do better at something. Parents need to guide a child to a realistic knowledge of the world and society. Families should not encourage unrealistic fantasies – an extreme example would be a tall,

overweight girl dreaming of being a prima ballerina and encouraged by her parents who know this to be an impossibility. A child needs advice on how the world works in reality not fairy stories

- a coherent set of values and ethics: a child needs to be introduced to the concepts of what is right and what is wrong and she will need parental guidance in making some decisions. A sound ethical grounding means a child will know how to act and know the right way to act: for example, she will be willing to help others, and will do unto them as she would be done unto.

THE DEVELOPING CHILD

Going to school

Starting school can be traumatic for some children. A child who has been cosseted at home with few social contacts with children of similar age may find the rough and tumble of the playground and classroom a rude awakening and his confidence may take a knock. However a child who has been prepared by attending playgroups and nursery and has learned to make friends (see Chapter Four) will have a head start.

A child with high self-esteem feels good about herself and expects others to have positive feelings about her. The contrary is also true. If you feel this is the case for your child, discuss ways of boosting self-esteem with the class teacher and follow the advice in this chapter, making sure your child has lots of confidence-boosting experiences and is praised for effort rather than outcome.

The older child

Self-esteem fluctuates throughout our lives, and perhaps never more so than during adolescence. Suddenly everything is wrong, from the shape of the nose, to height and hair colour. You name it and the young teenager will find fault with it!

A child who has previously enjoyed self-esteem will still have moments of doubt and may agonize over every perceived imperfection. That child is just as susceptible to the surge of hormones doing strange things around the body as a child who lacks self-esteem.

The poor self-esteem of other young adults usually makes them more vulnerable to feelings of aggression, self-doubt and marked moodiness accompanied by rebelliousness. Follow the guidelines above: it's never too late to improve a person's perception of self and boost his confidence.

The goal for parents is to help their child through this transitional phase by offering love, comfort, emotional warmth and consistency especially in a moral code.

Help your adolescent to feel good about her or himself by encouraging: good personal hygiene, exercise, a healthy diet and rest and relaxation, and as discussed above providing your unconditional love.

Summary

Making sure your child grows up feeling good about herself is one of the best gifts you can give. Children need to feel that they are significant and can have an effect on the world they live in. Being an only child does not automatically mean a child will have high self-esteem. It is the quality of parenting which counts in any size of family.

Part Two
Family Issues

Chapter 9
Two-parent families

I did feel lonely as a child. Both my parents worked from home and they were very involved with each other, hardly looking up from their desks when I got home from school. I don't feel I had much time to actually be a child because as soon as I could do anything for myself – like washing my own hair or making a meal – I was left to get on with it. I felt I was being pushed into independence before I was ready for it. Maxine, a marketing consultant

Two devoted parents and one child between them – bliss or a recipe for disaster? It can be both, although, as we have seen earlier, the only child is no more likely to be spoilt or over-indulged than a child with a brother or sister. No one can have too much love, it is when expressions of love become translated into material possessions and treats that problems may arise. Being loved and brought up by two warm, loving, emotionally suppor-tive parents is a wonderful start in life, having no set limits and being fought over or ignored is not.

A good relationship between parents and the child is in mathematical terms rather like an equilateral triangle: each side is equal. If the child or one of the parents is excluded or distanced then the triangle becomes an isosceles one, with two-sides equal and the family dynamics become less balanced.

The relationship between parents and child stands a chance of being at its optimum when both parents feel confident in their roles and each feels fulfilled and relatively happy with their life. Problems may arise if a parent feels he or she hasn't fulfilled their own potential and therefore may give too much attention to and be too demanding of their child.

It used to be that many women, feeling frustrated in their role as homemaker, wife and mother, devoted themselves to their children in a way which was inappropriate. Very often they wanted the child to succeed where they thought their own talents lay. If a mother had wanted to go to university but hadn't been able to she was likely to transfer her ambition for herself onto her son or daughter. This was fine if the son or daughter had the same goal in life but if not both parent and child were in for an uneasy relationship. If the mother was too dominant she succeeded in sending her son to university only to find once there he dropped out and started hitch-hiking around the world (if he was lucky!). In fact the son might not have been cut out for university life or may not have been ready to commit himself so by pushing him the mother achieved the opposite of what she desired.

These days the changes in the economic climate have meant that more men are unemployed and those who are in work often find themselves on short-term contracts and therefore have periods of time in the home. It is therefore equally possible that a man who is frustrated in his own life will pour his attention and the extra time he has at home on a child in the hope that he or she will succeed where he feels he has failed. His ambition is that the kudos and social status ultimately achieved by the child will rub off onto him.

Parents – of however many children – have to remember that although their child is a part of them, they do not own the child. Nor do they own the child's thoughts, hopes or ambitions and while it is helpful to offer advice and alternative ways at looking at things, it is brutally unkind to try to shape a child into your version of what you think he should be.

SEXUAL STEREOTYPES
Children without siblings tend to be less sexually stereotyped and therefore there is less need by the adults to have 'one of each'. A

single child combining the positive role characteristics of both sexes may satisfy the need to have more than one child in the hope of having one of each sex. Onlies tend to be more flexible in gender roles perhaps because parents of an only child have less traditional sex-role attitudes themselves. In larger families, parents tend towards the traditional pattern of mother at home with the children while the father is out at work. Even women who started out as committed to their career find that having more children tends to restrict them, as Frances pointed out.

> I went back to work after my first baby. My second baby was born two years later and while I was on maternity leave I was made redundant and I decided to stay at home for a while. Just as I was gearing up to look for another job I fell pregnant again – not intentionally. My partner in the meantime had got a much better job and I now find myself as the mum at home with the kids. The sort of jobs I could apply for are ones that demand flexible hours and that would be impossible with my partner's schedule. Also the childcare costs now would be too high and I couldn't face all the different arrangements I'd have to make. So it seems I'm destined to be the stay-at-home mum whose role is fairly traditional – I do the shopping, cooking, cleaning and gardening – and I must admit that I never envisaged this sort of role for myself and I do resent it at times.

The only boy

'Mothers tend to favour the only boy to a much greater extent than the only girl. There is some evidence that, while the close relationship of only children to their parents facilitates their need for achievement, it carries a risk also of too strong an identification with the parent of the opposite sex. Thus, there is a tendency for the only boy to be slightly more feminine than other males and the girl to be slightly more masculine than other females.' (M. Herbert, 1985.) This in no way affects the ultimate sexual orientation of a child and there is nothing wrong with girls developing their masculine side and boys exploring their feminine one. In fact it could be seen as a very positive development.

For the male only there is the chance that he will become a 'mother's boy' if his mother has no male partner or is unhappy in her relationship with the father. If her partner does not fulfil her needs, a mother may be tempted to channel her own emotional needs into her son who in turn clings to his mother's apron strings long after he should have given them up.

On the other hand, aware of this problem, a mother may be determined not to mollycoddle her son and may therefore not be as comforting or sympathetic when her son most needs her to be. She may appear very cold towards him as a way of protecting him and herself from an over-demanding and over-emotional relationship. Such a mother may insist that her son stands on his own two feet before he is ready to, leaving him feeling vulnerable and deserted.

A good parent will try to choose the middle path and be aware that there will be times when a son who refuses to kiss her at the school gate will suddenly need a lot more hugs and reassurance as he makes the transition from one stage of development to another.

The only girl

One comment that has been made about female onlies is that they find motherhood more difficult as they have no experience of babies or children and therefore find the whole experience daunting. I asked all my only girl friends if this had been so and for one, who hadn't particularly liked babies and thought she wasn't a 'natural' mother, this was one of the reasons she had an only daughter. However, many women do not find that being an only child is a drawback when thinking about starting their own families. One who went on to have four boys commented:

I had no worries about becoming a mother. However, I did check with a doctor first as my mother had lost several babies. When he said there was no reason for this to happen to me I went right ahead and had the four children I'd always wanted. I think I wanted four because I had been on my own but I hadn't suffered as an only. Where we lived in London there was always an aunt and cousins to visit. However although my parents came from big families, their brothers and sisters did not produce large families themselves. Three had none, two had onlies, one had two and one had three. Three of my cousins were a lot older than me and and three were younger and I often helped to look after them. When I married, I didn't think I was in any way ill prepared to be a mother.

Compared with girls who have siblings or only boys, only daughters may have more demands placed upon them. As discussed earlier, only daughters tend to suffer less from sexual stereotyping. They are less likely to be allotted a 'female' role and may be encouraged by both parents to tackle tasks that would normally have been the son's had there been one in the family. A father often passes on his skills to an only (or older) daughter and encourages her in so-called 'masculine' tasks. The problem only arises later in life, when the daughter is expected to achieve her career ambitions as well as find herself a partner and produce children. After all, these are the only grandchildren her parents will have. This may put an awful lot of pressure on an only girl, as Marie explains:

My parents always encouraged me in my studies and were terribly proud when I went to university. However once I embarked on my career there were all sorts of subtle digs about finding myself a nice husband and settling down. I resented this. Especially when they went on about grandchildren, as I knew only too well that I was the only one who could supply them.

I eventually married in my thirties and now have two boys. My parents moved to be near us and we see a lot of them. They are doting grandparents but sometimes I wish they had someone else to visit. On the other hand, they are always there for me and I don't have to share them as babysitters!

WORKING PARENTS
When both parents have an independent life outside the home, and bring new and fresh ideas to the family, a child blossoms. He sees both parents as fairly equal partners who both do important

jobs in his child's eyes. The problem for all working parents, regardless of the number of their children, is having enough time to do everything they need to.

As we have seen earlier some couples choose to have one child as there is less disruption to the mother's career and the father may have less to do, but having an only isn't necessarily an easy option, as one father commented:

> 'However tired you feel when you get home from work, you have to be there for your child. If he wants to play you can't just send him off to play with his brother, he hasn't got one. So you become the substitute. It can be exhausting.'

Many working mothers arrive home and have to start on the evening meal. This can be frustrating for a child who is dying to tell Mum all about his day or just wants a cuddle.

There are several ways round this. If your child has been at a minder's, where he has eaten supper you can delay your own meal to devote yourself to your child until his bedtime, and an older child who comes home from school on her own can make a snack for herself so that she can last out till a later supper time with her parents. Most people successfully work out their own routines which suit them and their lifestyle best. I have certainly found that forward planning meals so that you can buy ingredients and cook ahead if necessary makes life a lot easier, along with the odd take-away or restaurant meal to fall back on, and you can alternatively involve the child in the preparation of a meal. Young children love this, older ones will probably see it as a chore and are more likely to nibble and chat with you – if they enter the kitchen at all!

Working parents need to be well organized so that they don't miss out on their children and family life. Kate and Des are one such couple. Both have demanding jobs in local government but have made it a rule to spend as much time as possible with their son, Michael, who is now eight. Des begins his working day early so that he can pick up Michael from the childminder's at five in the afternoon. Kate starts later in the morning so that she can take her son to school. She then arrives home after the other two in the evening.

When Michael was a baby and I went back to work, we had Mary come to our home to look after him. At the time she had one child so Michael had some company. Just before Michael started school, Mary had a baby so we had to find someone else and this time he went to the minder's home. That wasn't as happy an arrangement so when he started school we found someone else who would have Michael after school and during the holidays. Dawn has her own three children at the same school and is wonderful. It means Michael sees what a family with more children is like and the boys have become like surrogate cousins now.

Des and I try to arrange our own holidays so that we both take some time off during the school vacations. Then we have some of Michael's friends round or take them with us when we go out. When we book our family holiday we involve Michael in our decision as much as we can. We have always made a point of one of us going to things like sports day and the school play and every now and again I do like to take a half-day holiday and help in Michael's class. It gives me an insight into what's happening in his life. I'm also involved with the parents and teachers association.

At weekends we spend a lot of time taking Michael to swimming and karate classes and ferrying him to friends' houses and birthday parties. We also make a point of seeing our families and Michael loves being with his older cousins.

Des and I share the domestic chores and food shopping fairly evenly which I think is important. Michael sees that we both work and we're both involved in the home. Our roles are not stereotypical and I think he'll benefit from that.

PARENT TRAPS

Parents competing for attention

When there are two devoted parents and only one child, it sometimes happens that one parent commandeers the major role in the child's life. If a mother doesn't have a job, she may find herself almost living through her offspring. However this syndrome is in no way confined to mothers, as Linda has discovered.

> When I had Holly, I didn't want to go back to work. At least not too soon. But financially it made sense and my husband, Peter, was quite adamant I should return. Obviously when Holly was a small baby I was very involved with her but I found as she became a toddler and from then on Peter seemed to take over. At first it was the presents he bought her. He insisted that only he knew what to buy and somehow I was never allowed to buy anything. I actually earn more than Peter but it looked as though all the good things and toys came from him. He would often come home from work with yet another toy, usually something he really liked as well!
>
> As she became school age he would take her out for the day, on her own, and she would come back with an expensive new dress or another pair of shoes. He seems to think that he should make all these decisions and I'm afraid I've let him get away with it for so long that it's become a way of life for us. I'd love another baby – although Peter has always insisted that we couldn't afford another – and I think that part of the reason is that we'd then have one child each.

Parents demanding too much attention

Another common pitfall for parents is that they actually want too much from their child. This of course can also happen in families with more than one child but with more offspring perhaps the need for attention is diluted.

This can lead to parents being over-involved when other children come round to play. Some parents of onlies want the children to play near them, want to feel involved, but it is far better for the children to go off and play on their own – as long as they are in a safe environment and can come to no harm. And it does give the parent a well-earned break to get on with something he or she enjoys.

Giving your child emotional independence allows for both true intimacy and separateness. If a relationship becomes controlling and engulfing it shows a lack of respect for the child's separate identity. This need to control leads to jealousies and is unhealthy.

The child as peace maker

It is never a good idea to involve children in any disputes between the parents, and this rule applies for any size family. However, when there is only one child there may be more of an inclination to confide in the child, to make an ally of her. This puts her in an invidious position which no child should have to face. Childhood is a precious time which shouldn't be invaded by adult cares and considerations. Until they are older, children can't understand why their parents fall out or argue. Their own experience of life is that people love them. A child cannot appreciate that love between adults is very different to the love a parent has for a child. In a family where there is a couple plus one child, the relationship can develop into a triangle which is far from equilateral when one adult pairs with the child. If the adult is of the opposite sex to the child the repercussions can be far-reaching. An over-strong mother–son relationship can affect the way in which the son ultimately relates to women and may impede him from sustaining adult relationships with the opposite sex. This is equally true of the father and daughter becoming close and uniting against the mother. In these situations a child has more power than she should expect to have and may become over-manipulative.

The child helps Mummy and Daddy too much

Another area which may be of disadvantage to an only child is one in which the child joins in helping Mummy and Daddy and therefore spends less time playing and getting on with childish things. This may be of more concern in a family with two working parents who, finding their own time at home restricted, may over-involve the child in household tasks and chores.

The child takes on adult worries

Only children are often seen as more grown-up, exhibiting more mature behaviour. This is a bit of a chicken and egg situation. What comes first: does being an only automatically make you more mature so that adults talk to you in a more grown-up way, or is it that only children are spoken to in a more grown-up way and therefore grow up quicker? Either way it is unkind to a child to allow him or her to assume adult worries.

Most children pick up on the moods of their parents, especially if they're anxious or distressed. Very often the child will blame him or herself (especially an only who has no sibling on whom to bestow this dubious privilege). If a parent does have worries (and who doesn't?) I think it's appropriate to tell a child without going into details. If you're tearing your hair out about imminent redundancy or a job interview, your child will notice and will worry. It's up to you, the adult in his life, to reassure him in a way appropriate to his age. If you've just screamed at your five-year-old for something that normally wouldn't bother you, apologize to her immediately and explain that all adults have things that worry them for time to time but that you will be able to sort it out. Part of growing up is to acknowledge that life isn't one long round of Disney World and ice-creams. On the other hand no child should carry a trunk full of adult problems on his or her shoulders.

Not taking time to talk

Many families find that they are so busy with day to day living and chores that they almost forget to talk to each other properly, to discuss things. Only children may sometimes feel excluded from the relationship between their parents and benefit from being included in conversations. Think back to when you last had a real conversation with your child if it was yesterday or today congratulate yourself. If you can't remember when as it was so long ago, make a conscious effort to improve matters.

One of the reasons we talk to our children less is perhaps because they or you are watching TV. It's not a good idea to start a conversation when he's in the middle of watching his favourite programme but the TV doesn't have to stay on afterwards. Once you get into the habit of sustained conversations you'll probably be surprised at the wit and wisdom of your offspring, who will often have you in stitches. As an entertainment, you couldn't find anything less expensive or more rewarding.

The wonderful thing about talking is you can do it in so many places:

- on the way to or from school
- over a meal together
- during a journey
- walking in the park
- after watching a film together – discuss it
- in the bath – if your child is young enough not to resent the intrusion
- at bedtime
- while you're preparing a meal
- while absorbed in another activity like painting or gardening

If as a family you are good conversationalists, your child will soon pick this up and initiate discussions. Make yourself available for conversations. If, however, the discussion seems important and is just about to start at an inappropriate moment, tell your child the time isn't quite right and ask to talk about it later, or in the morning or whenever (and make a mental note of it to yourself so that if your child doesn't bring the subject up, you can). My daughter is obviously well trained in this art. On the way to school with a friend I overheard her saying she was going to get a kitten. I interrupted (oops!) to say that she wasn't, to which she coolly replied, 'We'll talk about it later.'

If you find it difficult to start a conversation try asking questions that demand more than a yes or no answer, like 'How did you feel when . . .?' or 'What was your day like?' rather than 'Did you have a good day?' Ask questions like 'What was the best thing about school today?' and pick up on things that might be on-going, like a game that is currently in vogue in the playground or someone's health or the book he's currently reading.

SUMMARY

An only child in a two-parent family may feel excluded by the parents or equally may have a more powerful role, siding with one parent or acting as a go-between. For optimum family happiness a balance must be established and the child should feel she is an equal family member who is loved and respected.

Chapter 10

Lone parenting and the only child

My parents divorced when I was small and I was brought up by my mother and grandmother. I had loads of attention and affection and there is a very close bond between my mother and me. I never missed having a brother or sister. We lived in a remote village so my mother made the decision – which I think was very hard for her – to send me to boarding school when I was eleven. I didn't like it at first but if I hadn't gone I don't think I would ever have left that village. Being an only certainly made me grow up faster, I think. Sally, an editor in her mid-thirties

During both world wars while the men were away fighting for their country women were praised for bringing up children on their own. In fact some countries actively encouraged it. In Germany in the thirties, Himmler devised a policy to encourage young women of impeccable Aryan stock to have babies by SS officers whether they were married or not. If the young women were single and wanted to remain that way, provisions were made for them. They could, if they were so inclined, enter one of the special nursing homes Himmler set up and once they had had their babies they could have them fostered or adopted by good party members.

In Britain mothers brought up their children while often at the same time they were engaged in work outside the home, contributing to the war effort. Nurseries were often provided. With the war over and the men returned, the government wanted the women to return to their rightful place at home with the children, widows included. In many professions it was impossible for women to continue working after they married.

Our society has moved on since then but the respect and sympathy shown to widows bringing up children on their own has long since disappeared or at least diminished. Divorce rates have risen and lone parents have had a bad press during recent years. They have been blamed for producing criminals, delinquents, children who play truant from school and take drugs – almost anything that is wrong in society has been blamed on parents (for the most part mothers) who are bringing up children on their own, for whatever reason. In that climate it's difficult for the lone parent not to feel guilty and perhaps feel more vulnerable in relation to her parenting.

However, a lone parent should always bear in mind that there is never a single factor which produces a delinquent child. The government may blame bad parenting, or lack of a father figure who would instil a sense of discipline, but these are simplistic views which overlook the economic and social considerations it has itself created.

One of the main criticisms hurled against lone mothers who claim benefit is that the state is paying for their children's upbringing – not the father. What the critics conveniently forget is that there are now a million or so unemployed men who are claiming social security benefits for their children! In fact lone mothers with just one child are more likely to go out to work than lone mothers with more than one child and women in relationships who have more than one child, and of course there are a range or reasons why a parent is bringing up a child on his or her own: death of a partner, the break-up of a relationship or a conscious decision.

Sandra is an educated professional career woman who in her thirties decided to have a child by a donor.

I always wanted a child. I was a godmother to several kids and and spent a lot of time with them and liked that feeling and wanted more. I hadn't been in a relationship for a long time and decided to have a child on my own. It was really liberating to make that decision by myself and not have to take on board somebody else's wishes.

I never had an agenda to have more than one child partly because I was thirty-five when I had Rose. I felt that by having one I could keep the rest of my life going; having two would upset the balance. I can just manage financially by working three days a week and then I'm involved in a co-counselling group and I'm brushing up my French and writing skills.

I preferred a girl and am glad I got one. It's much easier to empower a girl, to teach her to be assertive, confident and so on, than it is to try and encourage female qualities in a boy.

Rose never asks about having a brother or sister. Sometimes I joke about having another baby and she looks a bit stunned. She doesn't see a lack in her life. We spend a lot of time with people with sole children. We go on holidays and stay overnight with a friend and her daughter. Rose and the daughter have a sort of sibling relationship – sometimes they fight and don't get on but generally they like being with each other.

My daughter is now six and I think it would be hard now to find and be with someone else unless he was very mature and was able to take on Rose and all that that entails. I couldn't put up with someone who went into sulks because he couldn't get enough of my attention. I don't think a male influence is desperately important. She has a comfortable relationship with a few men, like her grandad, and so far she has never asked any questions about her father. They don't seem to have crossed her mind yet although she is often with children who are in more conventional, traditional families.

If and when she does ask I have a box of things to show her including photos of her father who said he would be happy to meet her if she wanted to when she was eighteen. That's a bridge I'll cross when I get there.

For myself, I have to have adult space. It's quite important for keeping yourself sane. One thing I fight with Rose about is that she still comes into my bed at night. In many ways it's my *own fault because sometimes I'm just too tired to argue with her.*

I think only children are more independent and do more for themselves. Rose takes a grown-up interest in keeping the house. We do a lot of practical things together and she loves that.

So how do only children fare when brought up by one adult? There are no current statistics to determine the effects of being an only with one parent as compared to an only with two. However one aspect which must be considered is the financial one. Whereas a lone parent with one child is more likely to be employed, there is still only one salary coming into the home and childcare costs have to be met. With two parents there may not be two incomes but there will then be one person to fill the childcare role and therefore less money may be needed in the household budget.

Is an only child living with one parent worse off than two or more children living with a mother or father? A research study by Weiss in 1979 made extensive comparisons between single-parent families with and without siblings. The conclusion was that the one-parent/one-child family was less hierarchical but had less opportunities for mutual support and closeness with others. The child in such a family is more mature and receives more parental protectiveness and lacked an ally if the parents were in the throes of a divorce or separation. Only children in a single-parent family tend to be given fewer household chores than those with siblings, but that's possibly because with fewer people in the family there's less work to do. This is equally true in the case of two-parent families. More children seems to imply more chores for the children.

Less opportunity for moral support?

I think you have to be very alert to the fact that you might be going through a bad patch, be it at work, or physically or emotionally, and you must realize how much you are off-loading this on to your child who may have no one else to confide in. Most of the parents and children I have interviewed were fiercely protective of each other – even young children wouldn't hear a word spoken against their parents – but without another parent around to confide in, or a brother or sister to commiserate with, an only child can find herself isolated in her situation. I'm not suggesting that single parents become abusive to their children, rather that there are extra burdens attached to their lives that could cloud judgements from time to time.

One way round this might be to have another adult who is close to your child, who would listen to her sympathetically. I think as soon as a child can read numbers she should be taught how to use the phone, and perhaps she should be given a list of numbers she could ring in an emergency. Most children know about ringing the emergency services, but if their mother had collapsed in tears or was throwing their best dinner service at the wall what would they do?

Children benefit from having another adult to talk to whatever type of family they come from. Another adult can add a new perspective and it's handy to have someone else who'll take the child out to buy your Christmas or birthday present!

I'm not sure siblings can offer that much comfort, anyway. Young siblings are not yet able to communicate sufficiently, while older brothers and sisters may blame each other or come to conclusions that are far from accurate. Therefore another adult who is committed to and familiar with the child would be an appropriate source of support if and when needed.

Two's company?

Mother and child families tend to be cosy and sometimes too exclusive. The downside can be that such relationships can be too intense and a parent may view the child as a substitute mate. Weiss also showed that the mother and son relationship may be particularly strained by pressures on the son to assume a spouse-like role. This is not to say that a mother responds to her son in any sexual way but rather that she burdens him with her own problems and expects him to offer solutions. Comments like 'You're the man of the house now' or 'You'll have to look after

Mummy now' may sound quite innocuous, but to a young boy who will probably take them as literally true, they can impose an intolerable sense of obligation and responsibility which can be psychologically damaging.

Working parent

A working parent – in fact any parent who has wide interests outside the home – is less likely to make inappropriate demands on her child. She will introduce her child to the wider world and social context. Jayne is one such mother.

I have worked since my child was a few months old – it has never occurred to me not to. My relationship with the father broke up as a direct result of my pregnancy as he didn't want me to have a baby. However I wasn't living with him and I had my own home and was fairly well set up. If there ever is a right time to have a child I felt I had reached it and I have never regretted that decision. Being a working single parent means we have a reasonable life-style, we have holidays and I can afford treats from time to time. But sometimes being on my own takes its toll.

I do feel vulnerable on occasion and all the onus is on me. I have an income to earn, plus a house to run, garden to tend and of course a child who is always my first priority. The house can be in chaos, the kitchen a mess and you'll find me sitting on the floor doing a puzzle or playing a game because I feel that's more important than living in a Homes and Gardens setting.

I am very concerned that my child should not miss out on anything because he is being brought up by one parent. Perhaps that means that sometimes I try too hard and I can get anxious about everything from how he's doing at school to whether he's cleaning his teeth properly. I can usually see the warning signs, however, and I take steps to relax and talk things over with another parent.

Of course I've had to make sacrifices – what parent hasn't – but generally the things I've given up (like spending whole evenings in wine bars) have been no real loss. Now my son's needs whatever they be come first. However, I do make time for myself and have lots of friends I socialize with. I think it's very important for Josh to see that I have have a life apart from him and that he sees other families and how they work.

We have quite an extensive network of friends and although I have never joined a baby-sitting circle, I do swap child-caring. Now Josh is older, just nine, it's great fun to be able to do more adult things together. We often go to matinées at the theatre especially when there are special offers on. He is a great little companion and I'm aware of a temptation to introduce more 'adult pursuits' because they interest me. However, because I know this, I make sure there are enough trips to the park skate-boarding or kicking a ball around – he is still young and I'm not looking at him as a substitute for adult company.

I can truthfully say that the only things that really bug me are not being able to pop out and post a letter if he's in bed and not being able to nip down to the local pool for an early-morning swim. I shall have that to look forward to once he's old enough to be left on his own for a while.

However, I think once you have a child your view about work shifts somewhat. I used to do a lot of networking in the evening, which I've had to give up now. Also people do treat you differently once you've had a child – with or without a partner. At first they seem to treat you as though your brain has addled but that does improve with time. I'm also careful not to talk about Josh too much in the office. I take my cue from others. If they ask I show the odd photo and talk about his latest achievement otherwise it's very low profile.

As I don't have a partner, there's no one else to share the problem if Josh is unwell and can't go to school. So far it hasn't been a problem and I have a very good support network including my parents and his ex-carers, who will stand in if necessary. I think as a working single parent you have to be even more organized – you just can't leave things to chance. One half-term I was let down by everyone with whom I'd made an arrangement for Josh's care. I learned my lesson. Now he goes to organized play camps which are quite expensive but are *much less hassle. And the bonus is that Josh has a wonderful, active time swimming and playing sports and making new friends.*

PARENT TRAPS

The isolation of both parent and child

One of the disadvantages of being a lone parent with an only child is that you can become quite isolated and then you rely too much on each other for company. Having a child – even with a partner – can be an isolating experience if you're not in contact with other families. I think it's possibly easier to cope if you've always been on your own and have built up networks from the beginning, but that will vary from person to person. The strategies for building up your social life apply to everyone.

If you are newly separated, widowed or divorced and find yourself on your own with a child, life can be very difficult, especially if you have had to move homes. At first most people find they feel quite depressed, confused and isolated, and lack confidence. At the same time your child is probably feeling equally bewildered and unhappy. One recently divorced mother said:

> *The problem is how to cope with the special days. You know, Christmas, birthdays, even fireworks night. You want them to still be special and you don't want your child to feel that life has changed so much and make comparisons.*

It's vitally important for both your own and your child's well-being that you maintain as many social contacts as you can, especially with grandparents and aunts and uncles and close friends. This isn't always possible with some in-laws and friends who desert you when you need them most.

Special days need to be just as special when you are bringing up a child on your own. If you want to avoid comparisons with your previous lifestyle, treat special days differently. If you've always gone away for Christmas and now won't be able or invited to, invite people to your home. It doesn't have to be for the whole of the festivities – you can have a special tea or pre-lunch drinks.

Invite neighbours and friends you know will also be at home – it's amazing how many people are grateful for an invitation that will get them out of the house for a while and away from a disagreeable great-aunt or a father-in-law who has never heard of Christmas cheer.

Some traditions should be maintained if possible, and those are to do with your child. Children are amazingly conservative and hate change. Younger children may worry about Father Christmas being able to find them or if they'll get any presents at all. Talk to your child about how the festival you have celebrated as a two-parent family is going to be different this year and ask her what she would like to do. You might be surprised by some of the suggestions and find that they are easily put into practice.

> *My daughter and I had Christmas on our own last year. I was dreading that she might be disappointed but in fact we had a wonderful time. We went to church on Christmas Eve which is not something I would normally do but I wanted Gabby to feel part of a wider social context. In fact she saw lots of her school friends there, which made it rather special. Then we went for supper and drinks with another family. For Christmas lunch we set the table and dined in style, not making compromises because there were only the two of us. We both enjoyed ourselves, playing games and snuggling up on the sofa to watch a film. I was really touched when Gabby asked if we could do it like that again this year.*

Christmas, however, is only one of the many occasions when it's tempting to feel that all the world is partying except you. Rest assured: if you are on your own, there are plenty of others in the same situation. One way to avoid being on your own when you don't want to be is to visit a place where there are plenty of other people; a public fireworks display, a religious service, eating in a restaurant if you can afford it. The best way to avoid disappointment is to plan well ahead. Don't wait for invitations, issue them, and in plenty of time for people not to be booked up.

If you are normally not a particularly sociable person you will have to make a supreme effort for your child. Both of you need outside interests and stimulation. If your child is older and does have friends you don't want her turning down invitations because she's worried about what you'll be doing – if necessary say you have other plans (don't elaborate) and then she'll feel free to go off and do her own thing.

By going to the park and the local swimming-pool you can't fail to meet other parents and children, and it's relatively easy to strike up a conversation. If you're worried or unsure how to begin, complimenting an adult on their child's particular skill at diving or swimming or riding a bike is as good an introduction as any. Always give your own name along with your child's. If you say, 'I'm Anne, by the way,' the other person will probably respond similarly. If not don't feel affronted – he or she might be shy as well! On these occasions it is advisable to carry a pen and paper so you can give your telephone number or take down someone else's. Alternatively you could have a card printed. There is less chance that these will be lost and they are comparatively inexpensive and create a nice impression.

Other ideas on how to make friends are covered in Chapter Four and keeping in and maintaining contact with an extended family is explored in Chapter Eleven. You might also like to contact your local branch of Gingerbread, an organization for single parents (see the Yellow Pages).

If you're still in regular contact with your child's father, there may be times when he will want to have your child with him over a festivity or birthday. This is always particularly difficult for the parent who is left on his or her own. In these situations the needs of the child must come first. I can't imagine being without my own daughter on special occasions but a friend acted totally selflessly last year and sent her son to spend Christmas with his father who, because he now lived a long distance away, didn't see his son very often. 'He'll have a wonderful time,' she commented, and added that she'd make the most of it and go to a few parties herself. In fact she was ill all over Christmas and probably on her own most of the time. But just as she'd predicted her son came home full of his fantastic Christmas and seeing his dad's family, and happy to settle back with his mother. When he's older he'll realize what a sacrifice she made because she loved him.

Possessiveness

That mother showed a remarkable lack of possessiveness, but it's all too easy to fall into the trap of wanting to own and control your child. When you first have a baby it's only natural that you don't want to let it out of your sight. Some mothers can't bear someone else to cuddle the new arrival. It is the traditional role for the father to intervene gradually and return the mother's interest to the wider world. If you have been on your own during the early months you have to learn to let go and share your baby, for however short periods, with someone else. For your own good you need time away from a baby, even if it's just to have a bath or visit the hairdresser.

Possessiveness is not an endearing trait. Possessive parents can end up losing the son or daughter they were so anxious to keep to themselves. Emotional independence allows for both intimacy and separateness. A possessive relationship becomes controlling and engulfing and there is a definite lack of respect for the child's separate identity. This is an unhealthy state of affairs and may lead to the child being unable to form other relationships now and in the future.

The child becomes too old for its age

Two adult onlies told me that they did grow up quicker as an only child brought up by a lone mother. However there is no real empirical evidence to draw on. Who is to say that they wouldn't have matured early (if that was really the case) whatever their circumstances? Both onlies and first-born children tend to be more mature, the latter because they have often had to do things for themselves after the arrival of a sibling.

However, as parents we should be wary of a child becoming inappropriately old for her age. This may happen if the parent confides her worries to the child too much, or if the child spends too much time in adult company and not enough with children of her own age. A child who behaves too old for her age may find herself isolated from her peers either from their choice or because she finds them too immature. Either way she will be lonely.

Summary

A single child brought up by a lone parent is not intrinsically disadvantaged. As long as a parent is aware of the pitfalls and does not impose an adult way of life upon a young child, that child will flourish just as much as a child in a well-functioning two-parent family.

Chapter 11
Extending the family

'At Christmas there's only my mum and me, she's an only child too. I wish there were more people around, that we had a bigger family.' Amy, aged 11.

One of the major disadvantages of small families is that there are fewer people like uncles, aunts and cousins around to share the festivities and to socialize with. However much harried parents look forward to some peace and quiet, most children love being with other people. The problem is often more acute for the one-parent family (see Chapter Ten), when perhaps the child has only one set of grandparents and relatives to visit, but two-parent families can also find themselves in this predicament especially if they are only children themselves.

If you come from a large family with which you are still regularly in contact and have a wide circle of friends you'll probably want to skip this chapter, although I hope you will still find some useful tips for making the most of your contacts.

My own experience may illustrate ways in which a two-person family such as ours can be made to feel a lot larger. My family, like most others, has shrunk over two generations. Both my parents come from large families but they and their siblings have produced only one or two children each. Conscious of the fact that my daughter does not enjoy an extended family I have worked at creating one – a network of family and close friends who have a role in Olivia's life and will, I hope, be there for her if and when she needs them. Olivia doesn't see as much of her two first cousins as she would like (mainly for geographical reasons), but we have managed to enlarge our 'family' quite considerably.

When Olivia was born I asked four close friends to be 'godparents' (although we didn't have a baptism!). One of the four was my oldest friend, Chris, whose own two daughters Olivia considers as surrogate cousins. Another was Martyn, a cousin I'd kept in relatively close contact with, and he has been an uncle figure whom Olivia always includes in her increasing number of cousins. The other two are close friends, Morag and Marie, whom Olivia has grown up to regard as special for her even though they live a great distance away and she doesn't actually see them very often. In former times she would have addressed them with the courtesy title of 'auntie' but they're quite happy with the use of their first names.

Olivia also has some other special adults in her life. Fiona was my birth partner and was there for Olivia's delivery. She and her three sons regard Olivia as one of the family. Of the variety of carers Olivia had before she went to nursery at the age of two, Anna remained a constant and Olivia continues to see her and her family. Another friend of mine, Tricia, has become special to Olivia: she always remembers her birthday and sends her cards – like when she first started school. And so the net widens to include Sally and Alison who regularly collect her from school and other friends with children who have become regular visitors and companions.

And, of course, we also see my own aunts, uncles, cousins and their families from time to time, so that Olivia feels part of a much larger family and our small two-person unit has 'grown' so that there are always plenty of people around especially for special occasions.

The adage 'you can choose your friends but not your family' applies just as well to the size of family you were born into and the type of socializing that goes on between family members. You can't change who your birth family is or the size of it or the fact that some people just don't want to socialize or keep in touch. You can make the most of the family connections you do have.

When you first have a child the relationship between you and the young infant is exclusive. As the months pass, more and more people are included in your circle and that is how it should be. Just as children benefit from experiencing a wide range of activities so too is it advantageous for them to meet a wide range of people from different generations.

GRANDPARENTS

It can't have escaped many people's notice that along with Mother's Day and Father's Day, we now have Grandparents' Days, and there are even cards expressing congratulations on becoming a grandparent. Maybe this is because as a society we have lost touch with old traditions and ways. Maybe as a society we have ignored or undervalued grandparents – in many parenting books, for instance, grandparents are not even mentioned in the index – and these special days and cards are a small way of reminding us of the fact. Indeed it is only with the passing of the Children Act that grandparents have been officially recognized as having a right to see and to keep in touch with their grandchildren.

How grandparents are treated within families varies with different cultures and religions. In some communities the grandparents are expected to have rather a remote role, in others it is quite usual for the baby to be handed over to the grandmother. For instance in India, where the women work long hours on the tea plantations, it is the grandmothers who take care of the children during the day in nursery 'tents' set up near where the mothers are working. Hispanic families place a high value on the bonds within an extended family and the bond between a grandmother and granddaughter can be as strong as that between a mother and daughter.

Whatever your relationship with your parents has been, it changes subtly once you have your own child. In many ways it can be the last step into adulthood, and it certainly marks a turning point. You now have your own family, which takes priority. And yet it is at these times that you realize what your own parents have done for you, and recognize their love and the sacrifices they may have made. (This is also a time when many people who were adopted as children think about their birth families and consider trying to trace them.)

The relationship between a child and her grandparents if allowed to develop naturally is a very special one and they often find points of reference that have skipped a generation. For instance a grandparent who loves gardening, an interest loathed by his or her own offspring, may find a like-minded, green-fingered soul in a grandchild. Grandparents generally have more time to spare. Even if they are still working, they don't have the rigours of rearing children to contend with on a daily basis and are often more relaxed in their dealings with their children's children.

Grandparents offer another perspective on the world and they also have tales to tell – embarrassing or otherwise – about the child's parent when he or she was that age. They offer an early sense of history and continuum and are important in handing down traditions and cultural and religious values. This is particularly valuable for immigrant families in any society. A West Indian grandparent, whose own children may very well have been born in Britain, can tell tales of what it was like 'back home' especially if there is little likelihood of the child going there for some time. And it's so for grandparents from every culture and walk of life. Grandparents can provide an invaluable sense of history and perspective. Some will hold back and wait to be invited – so invite them; others will be on your doorstep at the moment of delivery. If that feels too intrusive, don't put them off too much. You'll want them involved with your child's life later on!

UNCLES AND AUNTS

One of the most joyful experiences in my own life was becoming an aunt and holding my nephew Daniel – himself an only for many years! – when he was just born. To say I adored him was a bit of an understatement and I enjoyed all the good things about having a baby in the family with none of the real responsibility – or the broken nights. Uncles and aunts can enjoy a wonderful relationship with their nieces and nephews and can be the supplier of treats and outings. They also provide another view of the world, and of your own family. There may also, as the child grows, be interests that an uncle or aunt may be able to help with, advise on or provide the wherewithal to follow.

COUSINS

It is often surprising to a brother or sister who did not get on when they were young that their own children rather like each other's company. Relationships between cousins have many of the benefits and similarities of those between siblings without the disadvantage of having to share their parents! As many sibling squabbles are really about competing for a parent's time or attention, cousins avoid this and often prove to be excellent playmates for each other.

For an only child, cousins can be a lifeline, especially in adulthood. A cousin may have remembered shared experiences, which helps promote a sense of continuity and a shared past that siblings enjoy. Cousins can be a great help when a parent dies as their grief as a bereaved niece or nephew is likely to be less intense. A cousin may be able to offer a more objective viewpoint – a help, for instance, when decisions have to be made about the care of an elderly parent.

Making contact and renewing contact

In many Western societies, as children grow up they move away from the family and see less of the extended family. Having a child offers an excellent reason for getting back in touch with people both family and friends.

- Send a card announcing the arrival
- Throw a welcome party
- Invite people to tea, etc.

If you live at a great distance from the rest of your relatives, make arrangements to visit one member of the family who would be happy to have others visit you there – that saves endless travelling with a small baby

BECOMING INVOLVED IN OTHER PEOPLE'S FAMILIES

Friends enrich our lives, offering other viewpoints, sharing experiences, then enjoying the good times and offering a shoulder to cry on when the need arises. There are many ways in which we can involve other people in our lives and participate in theirs so that a child will benefit from a wide and enriching social contact.

ADOPTING A GRANNY OR A GRANDAD

Just as small families may feel isolated and far away from their extended families, so older people miss their families and feel lonely. Friendships between generations who aren't related can be rewarding for everyone, especially when there is a child involved. Someone you've always nodded to and perhaps exchanged a few words with will often become suddenly far more friendly once a baby arrives and you may find a more fulfilling and pleasing relationship develops.

Helen, a nurse, recalls how one such friendship started for her.

> *I looked after George in hospital and we became friendly, talking about our families and that sort of thing – mainly because George seemed quite lonely as his wife had died and his children had moved away. My son Jake was about two then and I was really proud of all his antics and used to keep George amused with tales of them. When he came out of hospital, I realized he just lived a couple of streets away from me and popped in one day to see how he was managing. He was delighted to meet Jake and invited us back to tea.*
>
> *From then on the relationship developed and George has become a sort of extra grandad. He babysits for us on occasion and now and again he'll have Jake at his house while I go shopping. He comes to Sunday lunch about once a month now. He's really good with Jake and has so much patience with him. He teaches him little things about garden birds, which is one of his interests and about which I know virtually nothing.*
>
> *He feels like one of the family now and we have met his son and daughter and their families. They feel happier that their*

*father has someone¨else nearby — they have our telephone
number just in case they can't ever get through to George for
some reason and we have theirs in case of emergencies. We're
pleased to have his company, especially for Jake whose own
grandparents live quite a way away.*

Befriending an older person is really being a good neighbour,
checking they are OK during a cold spell or getting some
shopping in if they're unwell. You shouldn't impose your
company upon an older person and you should always be
sensitive to their need for independence and peace and quiet.
However your child will pick up the signals that you can care for
all sorts of people who aren't necessarily family and that it is part
of an individual's responsibility to society to look after the elderly,
who also have a lot to offer themselves.

MAINTAINING CONTACTS

The end of one relationship need not mean the end of any social
intercourse with other members of the family, and it's particularly
important that a child does not feel that she has been deserted by
one whole side of the family if her parents break up. This is
Joanna's experience:

*Both my parents are dead and my daughter Kerry doesn't know
her father's family as we broke up when she was very small.
However I did live with someone else after I broke up with
Kerry's father. Unfortunately that didn't work out either but
during that time Kerry had got to know Dave's mother and even
called her Granny. Dave was very violent towards me and when
he hit me in front of Kerry, I knew enough was enough.
However we have continued to see his mum. He went back to
live with her but she makes sure he isn't there when we visit and
really she's the nearest thing to a grandparent that Kerry has.*

OVERNIGHT STAYS

Overnight stays, if handled properly, are an excellent way for your
child to see how other families work and to get used to sharing
space with another child, to socialize and improve social skills and

cement friendships. The success of overnight stays for younger children depends on how well they are planned and catered for, the age of the children and your own expectations. While they are fun – hopefully – for the children, they are also an excellent way of sharing babysitting without having to wait up for the parent or parents to return after an evening out.

One of the major considerations in having another child to stay over is having the capacity to put her up. When you have one child you tend to buy things singly. I must admit I wish I'd been more far-sighted and had thought about buying bunk beds for my daughter. It's a major investment but once made you've always got a spare bed. As it is we bought a Z-bed that we refer to as our special bed for guests. Sometimes Olivia uses it, sometimes the friend.

When space is at a premium, a bed which pulls out from under the main bed is a good idea, as is a chair which folds out to a bed or an inflatable mattress. You will obviously also need some extra bedding or a sleeping bag. As sleeping bags tend to be popular with children, if you can afford to buy two do, the host child will more than likely want to use one too.

Another area where you may have to buy in a few extras is in the kitchen. If your child has special cups, mugs, bowls and glasses it makes life easier if you can offer a similar set to a guest. Larger families tend to accumulate these as a matter of course, smaller ones may need to buy in.

I think the first time your child stays overnight on his own is a major stepping stone on the way to independence. My own son was quite young – about three – when he stayed overnight with a close friend of mine who had a son of the same age. My son was used to getting up in the night and getting into my bed so I was quite interested to see what would happen when he was away from me – not to mention a little anxious. I was ready to go and collect him in the middle of the night if necessary. My friend had told her husband to go to the spare room if Ben came in to their room. However Ben slept through the night and really enjoyed himself both the evening before and in the morning.

Tips for younger visitors

- make sure the host knows any routine your child follows
- ensure that the child has any cuddly toy or doll he usually sleeps with
- tell the host parent of any particular food he hates or dietary requirements
- warn the parent if the child needs to a mattress cover in case of accidents
- leave a contact number especially if you will be going out during the evening

The first time I had a little friend of Lilly's to stay over was nearly a disaster – for me! The mother had told me that her four-year-old son Rory never woke during the night and was no trouble to get to bed. In fact he seemed to wake up crying every couple of hours and I found it quite difficult to get him back to sleep again. Eventually when he woke in tears at six thirty – and seemed inconsolable – I phoned his mother. By the time she arrived Rory and Lilly were playing happily and I had established why he had been upset. He was worried that his younger brother would be playing with his toys! I was relieved at that moment that my daughter is an only child.

The worst thing about having other children to stay is being unprepared for something. One child we had to stay was suddenly very tearful as he realized his mother hadn't sent his special milk with him for breakfast – he had an allergy to cow's milk. Once I'd assured him he didn't have to have cereal for breakfast and could have something else he cheered up.

Tips for having younger guests

Never assume the parent of your overnight guest will have remembered to tell you everything you need to know. Here are a few check points. Ask the other parent about:

- any routine the child has or likes to follow
- foods and drink which may not be acceptable

- the need for a mattress cover
- any health problems – many more children suffer from asthma these days and will need to have their inhalers just in case
- a telephone number to contact if they are going to be out

House rules

All homes tend to run on unwritten rules that have become accepted practice within a family (see also Chapter Seven). For instance one family might say that children should not play in the parents' room, jump on the furniture or turn on the television or video without asking; another family might be more concerned about taking outdoor shoes off in the home. When you have another child in your home – or when your child is in another environment – they need to know what the rules are. If your child is clear about the boundaries, then he will often tell another child not to go into a certain room, to take his shoes off or whatever. However, children do tend to forget themselves, especially when they have friends round to play, so it really is up to the parent to make sure the guest knows there are some rules and that they might be different to the ones at the other child's home. One example is using computers: in one home a child might be allowed to work on the computer unsupervised, in another the computer may be out of bounds unless an adult is present. As the children get older the house rules tend to evolve, perhaps giving more responsibility to the child. Some children tend to take their own family rules with them and wouldn't for instance dream of going into someone else's room without being invited to. Others happily forget the sense they were born with and run riot in other people's homes. It's better for everyone's peace of mind never to assume your child's guests fit into the former category!

SHARED HOLIDAYS

Taking a holiday with another family can be a lot of fun and if you are a single parent it's a way of decreasing the cost – few holiday firms give free child places when they are sharing with one adult. I have shared holidays twice with friends who also have only children and these have been remarkably successful. Once the children were the same age, and the other time the child was younger by about two and a half years – aged just like siblings might be.

In spite of the fact that we are supposed to use them to rest and recharge our batteries for the daily slog, holidays can be extremely stressful occasions. Parents who only see each other for a relatively short period of time suddenly find themselves thrown together for twenty-four hours a day; a child who normally has school and all sorts of other interests to occupy him may find himself more reliant on his parents for entertainment: being with another family means you can usually share the child-orientated activities between you and have some adult time too.

However, successful holidays don't just happen, they're planned, and if you are contemplating sharing a holiday, it's worth while discussing various aspects before you set off.

- self-catering: discuss how you will buy food, etc., and whether you will put money into a kitty and buy everything from that or perhaps divide the bills as you pay them.
- eating out: will you be paying for a child's meals or will he share the adults' portions? This can be a real bone of contention if one family is eating more than the other but only paying half the bill!
- bedtime: do you let the children run around until they drop, or are you going to impose a time for the children to be in bed by? This can obviously be negotiated on a more or less daily basis. Sometimes the following day's activities will mean you need an early night.
- ice-creams and treats: a quick discussion beforehand can prevent a situation in which one family has said no to something and the other has said yes.
- souvenirs: a similar situation; if you normally allow your child to buy a memento of a visit to a museum

or place of interest, mention it in advance so the other family is prepared.

- independence: this will depend on the age of the child, but you might want to allow a certain amount of independence. For example, if you're staying on a well-run, child-friendly camp-site you might allow your child to go off and buy the bread or milk from the camp-site shop. Discuss this in advance – the children might want to go together or to take turns. Whatever you decide make sure it is agreeable to both parties.

Taking a friend of your child's on holiday

I remember sitting on a beautiful rocky beach in Scotland, with lots of rock-pools and places to climb. Olivia was nearly six and was having a wonderful time but there was just one thing lacking – a playmate to share the fun with. Sometimes an adult just won't do. And it occurred to me then that perhaps it was time to think about inviting another child to accompany us on holidays.

Considerations for taking another child to share your holiday are similar for those to do with overnight stays, although you'll probably want to be better acquainted with the other child and his family before you embark on such an enterprise.

One way of testing out compatibility – yours with the friend as much as the two children together – is to invite the friend to join day outings and then perhaps a weekend before you set off for a week's vacation.

FAMILY TREES

Children love knowing where they come from, who their relatives are and how they fit in in the wider scheme of things – in the local community and so on – especially as they grow older. Although there are books on the market for younger children with titles like *All About Me* in which you fill in the relevant details and add photographs, I feel these can offer a negative image to an only child (and indeed to the child in a single-parent family who may not know one set of relations) in the sense that there are spaces which are not going to be filled in.

A far more positive approach, and a less expensive one, is to create your own book or draw up your own family tree or wall chart that shows the years and who was born and who they are related to and how. You can be as creative as you like, adding photos, drawings of the houses where people live or a large map to show where people live in relation to one another. This is particularly useful if some of your family live in different parts of the world. It can be something you do in an afternoon or a project that you work on for several weeks, depending on the age and concentration span of your child.

PARENT TRAPS

- Isolating your family from an extended one
- Failing to socialize
- Not reciprocating invitations for your child, thus eventually reducing opportunities for your child to socialize with other families

SUMMARY

All through this chapter I have been talking about ways to extend the family and the importance of widening one's net and sharing experiences with others outside the immediate family circle. However, that is not to say that there aren't times when you can enjoy being together with your child on your own. These times are very important too. A few days' break together, especially for families with working parents, when there's no one else to demand your attention is a marvellous opportunity to relax together, catch up on talking together and just enjoying being in each other's company. The breaks I take with Olivia are very different to when we share a holiday and I value them enormously. Although one friend of mine pointed out after a holiday in Portugal visiting her husband's family: 'Anna did enjoy herself while we were there, but once we were back home it was obvious she was far happier with her own friends. That makes you feel really wanted!'

Chapter 12
Becoming an only

I remember walking into the kitchen. My mother was sitting at the table and my father had an arm around her. I can still see this picture so clearly. Her chin was resting on her hand and I could see the the tears pouring down the back of her hand. It was the first time I had seen my mother cry. My father looked up, saw me and signalled me to leave the room. The door was shut very firmly behind me. And that's how I felt, shut out. No one wanted to know me or that I was grieving too. Mary, remembering the death of her sister when she was nine.

When people write about the birth order of children and the various advantages and disadvantages of any given position in the family, few mention the situation of the child who has become an only through the death of a brother or sister. Yet this has the potential for being the most difficult role of all, combining as it does all the negative aspects of being an only child and the least positive ones of having had and been a sibling.

There is always a special warmth, a special love for a child who has died. The earlier the death perhaps the greater the fantasies cherished by the parents, who may (consciously or unconsciously) pass these on to the remaining child, who grows up feeling second best and inadequate even when this has been far from the intention of the parents.

It may also be a surprise to parents that even a child who has never known an elder sibling who died may grow up worrying that he is not measuring up to what the other child might have been achieving. If the dead child was of the opposite sex a remaining boy might try to be more feminine, a girl might turn into a tomboy or try to act in a more overtly masculine way, parents might encourage this – whether intentionally or otherwise.

Children acquire all sorts of ill-conceived ideas from half-overheard conversations and odd remarks between adults. Parents need to acknowledge that children may pick up and absorb the wrong ideas about themselves, leading to all sorts of problems in later life, if they do not have the truth explained to them.

CONFRONTING DEATH

Talking about death to a child is one of the hardest things to do, especially when you are grieving yourself and probably in shock. At those times we often clutch at clichés, or try to explain things in a way that often rebounds on the grieving adult. When I was about three-and-a-half my maternal grandfather died at home. His body had to be removed and as I was far too curious for my own good my mother and grandmother were trying to persuade me to go out and buy some sweets with an aunt while the doctor came 'to take Grandad to heaven to be with Jesus'. I was obviously very impressed and immediately suggested I should go and see Jesus too and then come back with the doctor. Death probably seemed very exciting to a small child and this scene illustrates how easy it is to tie yourself in knots when trying to explain difficult concepts to children.

However, it's one thing to discuss the death of an old if beloved grandparent and quite another to face up to talking about the death of an infant or child. We don't expect children to die and their deaths are often all the more painful, all the more harrowing, and because of this we tend to avoid involving the surviving child in the grief process, as if by not including the child we will prevent her from being upset or sad. It's a real ostrich mentality. If we refuse to speak about death and dying and sweep the subject under the carpet, it implies to our child that that is the way to deal with the unpleasant realities in our lives. A child might also get a totally contradictory impression and think that the dead child is 'out of sight and out of mind' as far as his parents are concerned, and this may lead him to believe that they didn't really love his sibling and, by a process of infallible deduction, that they don't really love him either! None of it is true, but you can see how misconceptions develop.

It is only relatively recently, with marvellous discoveries and developments in medical science, that our life expectancy has extended into the eighties and nineties and so few children succumb to infant mortality. In the previous two centuries often as many as three out of four children christened died before they had reached the age of five. The situation is now similar in areas of famine and war in the Third World. Where the incidence of the death of babies is high, parents have to take a more practical attitude, sometimes having to make a choice between one life and another, one child and another. In Western society, where infant mortality is low, we often find ourselves unable to come to terms with the death of a baby or a child and find it virtually impossible to discuss this with another child.

In many cultures children naturally learn about death and the rituals to honour a dead person and send him or her splendidly on their way. In British society we seem to have lost that art. Children are kept very firmly out of the way and few are even admitted to visit a dying relative, let alone attend a funeral. Yet these things are important to facilitate the grieving process. If a child just never sees a brother or sister again, his or her death will be all the harder to comes to terms with. Just as do some adults who have lost members of their family during a war overseas, they expect the dead child to walk back into their lives at any moment.

If a child suffers a long illness, the remaining sibling will often feel cut off, alone, hurt and resentful. It probably feels as though her life is put on hold while all the parents' energy and commitment are directed towards the dying child with scant thought to the living. The child should, if possible, be included in the visiting and should be allowed to talk to the dying sibling and perhaps help with little practical things like making sure she has enough change for the phone if that is appropriate or buying her favourite comic. A sibling may be able to relieve the boredom of a hospital ward and at the same time give some respite to the parents.

While we prepare our children for living independently, we give little attention to educating them about dying. And those parents who do, sometimes do so in a rather oblique way. In my local pet shop the owner was asked how long a gerbil lived for. When he replied about two years, the man said, 'Great, that'll do to teach them [his children] about death.' And that very often seems to be the extent we teach our children about mortality – relying on animal deaths. In fact parents often judge what they think a child's reaction to death will be by the way they behave when a beloved pet dies. Sometimes a child will seem quite unmoved, as Jessie was when her gerbil died – she seemed quite pleased and asked if she could have a kitten now to replace it. However, twelve-year-old Don was inconsolable when his cat died and his mother blamed herself for allowing him to be part of the decision-making process in ending his long life at the vet's. Paula felt guilty that she had imposed so much grief on her only son but she was wrong. Don worked though his grief, he talked about it and he expressed it in his tears and eventually after a couple of weeks he came to terms with it. It was an excellent preparation for facing the other deaths which will inevitably follow.

Even a young child may feel intense grief when someone who is important and close to them dies, and this is particularly true of a sibling's death. Then, rather than minimizing or dismissing a child's grief, we should try to help her to understand and come to terms with it. By talking about the death and expressing our own feelings and ideas simply and honestly and listening to the child's own thoughts, adults can help a child come to terms with a death.

People with religious convictions have a framework within which to discuss death. Those without a formal faith might like to say that the spirit, the essence of the brother or sister lives on in the family she loved. These days we usually have a mountain of photographs of our children and it sometimes helps a sibling come to terms with her loss to compile a special album of her own with photos of her sibling at various ages and times in her life.

Blame and responsibility

Children often blame themselves for someone's death even though they can have had no possible connection with it. It is even more probable that this will happen with the death of a sibling. How many times do brothers and sisters shout, 'I hate you, I wish you were dead!' Even if they don't actually articulate the thought many siblings wish a brother or sister dead and certainly nightmares about killing off a sibling are common (deaths of parents are also usual!).

A child needs to know that he is not in any way responsible for his brother or sister's demise and he should never be made to feel guilty – however inadvertently – for surviving. Chrissie's family suffered three tragedies but her parents, in the midst of their own grief, managed to allow their only daughter to come to terms with the deaths and continue living in a positive and happy environment. However, they did find it more difficult to give her her independence.

I was the survivor of baby twins. I never thought a lot about it because I hadn't really experienced having a sibling although my mother was a twin and she always had a good relationship with my aunt and we lived together with her and her only son for a time during the last war. I was nine when my brother died at eighteen months. It was very sad. I still remember the baby. When I was fifteen, I had a sister who was born dead and that was very traumatic for my parents. I think it probably made them more attached to me. They wouldn't let me go, really – even when I married and had my own children.

Deaths in the family

Compare Graham's and Mark's reactions to the death of a brother.

Graham's brother committed suicide when he was a teenager. It was an act the family was unable to come to terms with and Graham, now in his forties, still feels angry with his brother and angry that his mother still phones him up and gets upset on the anniversary of his brother's death. He sees the suicide as an act of betrayal and an act of cowardice and refuses to consider that he might be depressed by it. That would be tantamount to revealing what he sees as his own weakness – how ineffectual he felt in preventing his brother's death. This is a very common reaction to suicide and he really blames himself when he shouldn't do. Mark's brother died at the age of nine from cancer.

*My mother tried to make my childhood as normal as possible.
My brother's death was obviously traumatic for us all and I felt
it very deeply but my parents were marvellous with me and we
worked though it as a family. I think that experience has made
me much more sensitive to other people's problems.*

Learning how to mourn

Denial of grief may lead to overcompensation in adult life. A child
must be allowed to mourn. If this doesn't happen then in later life
she may overreact to sad situations or in the face of another's grief.
Losing a brother or sister is a very sad event in a child's life, but
sadness is a part of life and we have to learn how to cope with it
and not repress it. Being frightened of sadness may mean that you
use all your energy trying not to feel it and therefore take years to
come to terms with your loss – a lot longer than if you had
mourned at the time. On the other hand you must not confuse
sadness and mourning with self-pity. Robin Skynner summarizes
the difference between the two thus in *Life and How to Survive It*
(1993): 'You have to distinguish between sadness and self-pity
. . . Grief is when you accept loss . . . You let the pain act on you,
let it change you. Then it forces you to let go. By contrast self-pity
is what you feel when you don't accept the loss . . . you want to
put the clock back as if the loss hadn't happened.'

Perhaps this can be illustrated best by the family which has a
child who dies but goes on to have another child and use the
experience positively. TV presenter Anne Diamond, who lost one
of her sons through a cot death and has used her own experience
to help others, actively campaigning for more research and better
information, is an example of someone who has accepted her loss.
The self-pitying family cannot accept its loss and tries to blame
others for its misfortune: it becomes in effect martyrs to its own
cause.

Telling a child about a miscarriage, stillbirth or neonatal death

Women who suffer early miscarriages often haven't told their
child about the pregnancy so are saved an explanation about a lost

baby. You may, however, need to explain a stay in a hospital or the fact that you are very sad and a bit tearful to a confused or bewildered child. Saying that you've been unwell but are getting better is probably explanation enough for most children. A younger one will probably respond well to being told, 'Mummy needs a lot of hugs and love at the moment.'

However explaining that a baby who has been eagerly awaited was born dead or died soon afterwards is a very different thing. Sometimes even the medical profession can't explain why a child was stillborn, so don't always try to find reasons, just explain the facts as gently and honestly as you can.

Very young children will accept a very simple explanation and what you say depends very much on your cultural or religious beliefs. However, while it is relatively easy to explain that someone who was old and very ill has died and is now at peace, happy, in heaven or gone on to a better place, it's virtually impossible to reconcile a loving god with the death of a baby or young child. Children are very literal and may react quite negatively to the idea that a god has chosen the baby to be with him.

By the time children are four or five and are asking endless questions you may find that if you have said the baby has gone to heaven you will be cross-examined about where it is, who lives there and whether anyone can visit, and as you'll be shocked and grieving yourself this is the last thing you'll need. Ask the child how she feels about what you have just told her and suggest that she might have some questions she would like you to answer. Be prepared to discuss the death over and over again until the child absorbs what she needs to and lets the matter drop.

PARENT TRAPS

Allowing the survivor to feel second best

No child should grow up under the illusion that he is not as good as a brother or sister. When this sibling is in fact dead, it is even more soul-destroying for the survivor. A dead child may have been idealized by the grieving parents, with imperfections long forgotten. If the dead child was older, the remaining child may have only a hazy memory of him anyway and will at some point achieve the age the dead child was and continue on. Beyond this time there is nothing to compare with and it is unforgivable for a parent to say things like, 'I think your brother would have done it this way . . .' or, 'I'm sure your sister wouldn't have spoken to me like that . . .'

Failure to accept and deal with a child's grief

Children do need to express their grief and sadness in order to come to terms with it. Many adults assume that a child just gets over a loss without much help, but children can experience profound grief and if no one acknowledges this they will repress it and perhaps suffer psychological problems. You will all need to talk about the dead child, to honour and remember him, and your surviving child will need to be a part of this mourning ritual.

Overprotecting the surviving child

If you have lost a child through accident or illness, it may be tempting to cling on to a remaining child in a sort of desperate bid to make sure nothing happens to her. This is a very natural reaction but one that needs to be nipped in the bud. You cannot, in looking after your child, make provisions for every eventuality – just as the King in 'Sleeping Beauty' found: he thought he had got rid of all the spindles but one remained and that was all that was needed to send his daughter to sleep for a long time! You will only alienate your child and make him resent your interference in his life.

Transferring goals for a dead child on to the survivor

When a sibling dies the survivor's relationship with the world changes subtly – he or she no longer enjoys the role of brother or sister. In the past the laws of inheritance favoured the first-born; if he died the sibling was automatically elevated to a new status, that of heir. A member of the aristocracy would suddenly find his whole life plan had changed from being a second son with a prospective career in the army to becoming the next lord of the manor.

This can happen today in different ways. Parents may have had high hopes for the child who died – maybe she was particularly gifted musically, or was destined to be a doctor – and seeing these hopes thwarted in one child transfer them to the survivor. No child can replace or stand in for another and it is unfair of parents to want them to.

SUMMARY

A child's grief at losing a sibling should be acknowledged and parents should ensure that the surviving child does not assume the blame for the loss. A child growing up feeling guilty that she survived when a sibling didn't needs to be shown she is important and unconditionally loved. Counselling by an expert may be advised. However sensitive parenting will ensure that a child comes to terms with her grief and feels good about herself and her role within the family.

Chapter 13
No longer an only

'Of course, it's a terrible come-down for the eldest when the second child arrives. I was the eldest of five boys. And I certainly do remember that. There's a feeling of sunshine and bliss in connection with the first four years, until the brother next to me arrived, and then it's as if a bomb went off, and after that for a long time the feeling is grey and dismal . . . I also think my family had a fear of jealousy . . . Therefore they tried to stop me being jealous by giving in to me, when they would have done more good by drawing firm lines within which I could learn to cope and gradually get over it.' Robin Skynner, in Families and How to Survive Them (1983)

A SIBLING'S ARRIVAL

A child who has been an only for some years may see the arrival of a sibling as a very mixed blessing. When he's been an only for all his preschool and infant years, it may come as quite a shock; by this age he usually has a fairly active social life with all sorts of extracurricular commitments. For the parents of a new baby the upheaval may be quite traumatic, and all sorts of plans have to be rescheduled, as Sue, whose son Daniel was seven when she had another baby, found.

We were actually on the point of emigrating to the States when I discovered I was pregnant. It was a bit of a shock. We were all packed up and everything. However, the baby changed everything. I didn't feel we could go as I was the one who had a job to go to and now wouldn't be able to work – my husband was going out there to look for work. So in the end we decided to trade our ticket for returns and have a three-week holiday instead. We went to Disney in Florida, which in retrospect was a bit of a mistake as Daniel thought that was the States and he would have lived in that paradise. He has actually said, 'Oh, Katey, why did you have to be born just then? You stopped us going to this wonderful land!'

I did want another baby and I was over the moon having a little girl. Daniel was always very good with other people's babies and he was good with Katey. But he did feel jealous though it wasn't so obvious as in a younger child. As Katey got older, he used to give her little pinches or whatever.

Daniel did enjoy being an only. He is very much a 'look at me' child but that's his nature, not a result of being an only child. I'm an only child myself and I'm not like that at all. He has a very demanding and outgoing nature but also has a very soft, loving side; from when he was little he had a very strong maternal side to him. A French friend of mine said he's not like a typical English boy.

As an only child we never had any problems with him because we were aware of the pitfalls. However, when I had another baby, people said, 'That'll do him good,' as though having a sibling would change his personality and that by implication it needed changing. It didn't on both counts.

I did a lot with Daniel when he was young and once Katey came along there was a feeling that we couldn't just get up and go any more. I did keep explaining things to him and I tried to keep up his social activities. She really had to fit in more with him after school. But there is a pull between the ages. In the evenings I always make time for Daniel who's now twelve, as he needs help with his homework, or practising for tests. Katey gets quite jealous and tries to interfere sometimes – that's the problem with having two so far apart in age.

Katey does try to keep up with Daniel and there's still a lot of rivalry between them. They compete for everything (she complains that he's got the bigger bedroom and so on) and Daniel always descends to Katey's level. When they are fighting and squabbling I do end up stressed, I suppose because I never experienced it myself.

THE EFFECTS OF DIFFERENT AGE GAPS

Research shows that children under five are more likely to be affected by the birth of a sibling. However, as the first few months pass, it doesn't seem to make much difference whether the age gap is small or large.

However much you promise yourself that the new arrival won't interfere with an older child's schedule and social activities – rest assured she will! As soon as the baby is born she will seem so tiny and vulnerable compared to your older child that all your maternal instincts will initially be towards the new infant. This is where a father or another committed adult can make the transition more bearable for the ex-only by being involved in her life and making sure things are continuing smoothly at school and with any other activities.

GOING FROM ONE TO TWO CHILDREN

Making the transition from a one- to two-child family needn't be traumatic but you do have to work at it. A first-born child will experience feelings of jealousy and resentment at times and it is up to the parent to define the limits of acceptable behaviour and help the child remain within them. Some children will need a lot of extra hugs and comfort, others will be happy and confident to hug the baby. In most cases the older the child the easier it is to welcome a new sibling – as long as the baby doesn't affect his routine too much!

Remember the older child: a checklist

During the first few weeks after the arrival of a new baby, it's very easy to forget that the older child still needs your love and protection and may feel a little resentful as well as bewildered by his own feelings. So:

- don't give too many chores to the older child
- don't turn the older child into a babysitter
- don't expect the older child to give up his activities because of the baby, try to accommodate both children's needs
- try to keep some time for you and your older child to be together (perhaps when the baby is sleeping or when you hand him over to the father)
- try to keep up to date with everything that is happening at school – do your best not to miss a parents' evening or a concert your child is involved in
- if possible let the older child keep his own room: nothing is worse than trying to share with a much younger child

ADOPTING ANOTHER CHILD

Marie Stopes, the celebrated advocate of birth control, had one child, a son, but, wishing to provide him with company, set about in a rather high-handed way 'adopting' boys of a similar age to be his companions. These boys didn't seem to last long and they were made very aware of their secondary importance. If the son was given a play suit of armour, his would be almost authentic while the adopted son's would be made of cardboard!

Hopefully no one would contemplate such actions these days but it has to be stressed that a child who is adopted into a family is likely to arrive with a trunkload of problems which will take a very special and sensitive family to accommodate. Linda did consider the possibility.

Adoption had always been an option in my mind and when my son was coming up to school age I discussed the possibility with my husband, who had always been lukewarm to the idea anyway. When he realized the type of background a child who was up for adoption might come from he definitely decided against it.

There are lots of factors that have to be considered when adopting a child, just as there are numerous needs of the prospective adoptee. Sometimes social workers will want a child to go into a family where the existing child is older or younger – not of similar age. Many children will have special needs. Some will want to keep in touch with their birth families. The British Adoption Society produces a newsletter called 'Be My Parent' and also an excellent booklet which introduces prospective adoptive parents to the philosophy behind their adoption policies (see the Useful Addresses section at the end of the book).

BECOMING A STEP-SIBLING

You might think that when two only children are brought together in a new family, sparks will fly: two children used to holding centre-stage having suddenly to share the limelight seems a recipe for disaster. However as we've seen from parents' experiences throughout the book, most only children are brought up by adults who are very aware of the pitfalls of being an only child and who have followed strategies to ensure their child will not be a 'spoilt, selfish, maladjusted' child.

Linda and Paul have been married four years. They each have an only child from a previous marriage. This is how they coped with introducing two onlies to the concept that they had a step-sibling.

Linda had met Carol, Paul's wife, at a playgroup and became friendly. Her own relationship with her daughter's father broke up and not long afterwards Carol left Paul and their son Liam.

There was never any question of Carol taking Liam with her. He just wasn't part of her plans. I began looking after Liam while Paul went to work so the two children knew each other from a very early age. Paul and I fell in love and we married when the children were about five years old. Both children found it hard to come to terms with the fact that they now had to share their parent. They were both clingy and very sensitive. I think they were worried that as they had already lost one parent they could just as well lose another.

Very early on Paul and I made decisions about what we would accept in terms of their behaviour. For example, both used to hate to see us cuddling and showing affection and always used to push us apart but we agreed they had to see us being loving towards each other and encouraged them to join in a hug.

The jealousy between the two children didn't last long but they do assert their own personalities. They're completely different. Liam is very easy-going and likes to have fun while Isabel is very thoughtful and likes to moan a lot, but they're both strong-willed. I have never said go away and sort out your own problems. I've always been very much a hands-on parent and encouraged them to talk to me about their grievances and why their feelings are hurt.

The worst problems have really been from all the extra sets of grandparents. The children were pulled about emotionally by others in the family. My family accepted Liam as my son. But Liam's maternal grandparents wouldn't accept Isabel.

They would send Christmas presents for Liam and nothing for her. At one time there was a huge difference in the number of presents they each received. To get round this I asked Liam's mother to keep the presents her family sent for Liam at her place.

The children go to the same school but are in different classes. I changed Isabel's name by deed poll so we would all have the same name. We did talk about adopting each other's child but decided to leave it as it was for the time being. In the beginning Paul and I used to row because I thought he was being too soft on Isabel and too hard on Liam. I'm sure I overcompensated as well. In a way it was easier for Isabel as she was definitely looking for a substitute father as she hardly ever saw hers. Liam was different. He used to shout that he hated me but now he calls me mum as well. I think I made the mistake of thinking I could replace his mother which of course you never can, even though she went away and left him. Really I had to learn that I was his step-mum.

BECOMING PART OF A NEW FAMILY

Morag was a single parent and Leah, her only daughter, had never met her father or his family. When she was a year old her mother met Nigel who gradually became more and more important in their lives. Leah had always addressed Nigel as Didi and when the couple eventually married, Leah carried on with the name.

As Leah got older I told her she had a birth father who wasn't Nigel but she didn't really seem all that interested. In her mind Nigel has always been around for her and they get on really well together. I had Eleanor when Leah was nearly five and, like many children, she didn't react very well to the new arrival. Although she was always lovely to the baby she was just unpleasant to me and often unruly. It took her a while to adjust to not having my undivided attention. Eleanor is three now and they've both settled down. In the meantime my ex-partner's daughter got in touch and has met Leah once. So now Leah knows she has some half-siblings as well and is part of a much bigger family.

Points to consider when an only child and parent are incorporated into a new family with a child or children:

- give all children time and space to adjust to the new set-up
- if you are moving into the home of one half of the new family, it is important that the 'resident' child or children don't feel pushed out and that the incomers feel welcome and that they have an equal stake; best of all set up home in a new house
- don't expect children to love each other and get on straight away – if they all end up liking each other it will be a major achievement
- as a new couple, decide on behaviour that is acceptable and unacceptable to both of you and make sure all the children understand the house rules
- if feasible let the biological parent do the disciplining – if the step-parent is always seen as the one who tells you off it imparts too much of a negative image
- if you hear the children arguing or fighting, don't rush in to arbitrate, give them time to sort it out for themselves: the chances are that they will learn to do this quite quickly
- bear in mind that biological siblings are always falling out, squabbling and then being the best of friends
- make time to be with your own child and try to ensure that her social life isn't totally disrupted by the new family arrangement
- read the section in Chapter Fourteen on step-parenting an only child

THE YOUNGEST CHILD ONLY

At the other end of the spectrum is the 'only' child who is so by virtue of the fact that she is born so many years after her older brothers and sisters. Sometimes the siblings are grown up but in all events they are older by a minimum of seven years.

This child is in the rather ambiguous position of having so many older people to care for her – and indulge her. A late baby is often cherished by the siblings as well as the parents, as Joanna recalls.

> *I was younger than the next child by ten years and my brothers were almost old enough to be my father. In fact one of them had a daughter only six months younger than me. It was a curious mix of generations but I never felt that my mother was particularly old – although she was in her mid-forties when she had me. I grew up with lots of family around so I never felt lonely. I suppose my dad indulged me a bit with nice clothes and shoes or whatever but I don't think I was spoilt or made to feel extra special or anything. The worst thing about my own situation is that all my family have now died and I'm left on my own. Although I do have my own family I still miss them.*

PARENT TRAPS

- too much babying of the last child
- overindulgence
- not allowing the child enough independence
- giving the child too much independence – expecting her to grow up quickly because she has older siblings
- making a child feel too special
- feeling weary of parenthood and not helping your child to socialize

SUMMARY

The arrival of a sibling or step-sibling after years as an only child may disrupt the balance of the family for a while. However the fact that the former only child is older usually means that the addition to the family, sensitively handled by the parents as well as friends and family, is accepted without too much trauma and seen as an enriching experience.

Chapter 14

Becoming the parent of an only

I know my stepfather cares about my mother and that's good. But I'm sad about two things. One is that my father hasn't remarried, so my mother is one up. And also the realization that my mother wasn't really happy on her own . . . When they're alone, everything they do is for you. When they remarry it's for themselves. Sophie, eighteen

Becoming a parent is a difficult enough transition for anyone to make. However much you plan, read about parenthood and try to prepare yourself, the birth of a child is always a shock to the system and your life is never the same again. Becoming a parent to somebody else's child – when you haven't had a run-up to the event – can be a minefield which should only be entered into by the strong and determined.

Assuming a parental role to a child of whatever age without the benefit of a pregnancy which helps to prepare you psychologically for parenthood, may mean an enormous amount of reassessment of one's life and readjustment for someone who may never have been married before and who may have had little practical experience of children. Children are noisy, time-consuming and expensive, play havoc with your emotions and are physically draining. So it's perfectly normal for a man or a woman with no experience of being a parent to feel resentful. And there's no law which says if you fall in love with someone you'll automatically love their child. For many people embarking on a new relationship, a child is often regarded as an acceptable inconvenience and at worst a major drawback. But

161

once a relationship is established, the step-child can be a positive bonus.

Step-parenting

The role of a step-parent has acquired some negative connotations which have to be overcome. Wicked step-parents abound in children's literature but are actually a relatively modern device to make vice and abuse in families seem more palatable and less 'unnatural'. Thus the evil is always perpetrated by a step-parent without the natural parent being aware of it, as in 'Snow White', 'Hansel and Gretel' and of course 'Cinderella'. Children's writers these days have tackled the subject more sensitively and show step-parenting in an altogether more positive light, without denying problems which may exist and show- ing how families can work through them to the benefit of all parties. This reflects the make-up of our society: with one in three marriages ending in divorce the step-family is becoming increasingly familiar.

How easy the transition is from being Mummy or Daddy's friend to becoming a resident step-parent depends on many factors, such as the age of the child, the family circumstances and the personalities involved. A step-parent may also have unreal expectations of chil- dren. If he or she has no child of his or her own, then the opportunity for learning about childcare has been reduced, and the new parent will have to learn 'on the job'. If you're struggling to come to terms with your new role and wondering how anyone else copes, it is worth remembering that the problems may not be of your own making; you can be stuck with the absent parent's parenting mistakes.

A step-parent may also assume he or she is more important in the child's life than is actually so. There may be a whole range of other adults like grandparents, uncles, aunts, friends of the family and teachers who may be more or less important in the child's life. This can have a rather humbling effect on the step-parent who may have nurtured an idea of a rather more impressive role, only to be met with a walk on part!

When the absent parent is dead

If the absent parent has died, much will depend on how his or her death was explained and how long ago it all happened. Of course the dead parent will and should be talked about, and contact should be maintained with that part of the family. No step-parent can ever replace a biological one but you may find that the dead parent has been idealized, making him or her a hard act to follow. However you must persevere and allow the child to see that you have much to offer as well – maybe in different areas.

> *My dad died when I was eleven. My step-dad's brilliant. He said he'll never try to take the place of my dad. I couldn't call him dad though I'd like to.* Nadia, seventeen

WHEN A PARENT HAS LEFT

> *I used to blame my step-dad for my parents getting divorced and I used to hate him so much. Now I really like him!* Lucy, fourteen

Even if your relationship with the parent began well after the marital breakdown, a child may still blame the step-parent, thinking that if this new man or woman wasn't there then her real parents could and would get back together again. However unrealistic this hope is, many children will still cherish it as an ideal well into the new family's life together.

At the same time a child may blame herself for a parent's absence (even if the parent is dead) and will feel guilty. The child should be encouraged to talk about her grief, unhappiness and fears, and have them put in context by a sensitive adult. Be as reassuring as you can and be aware that the child is now going through another painful situation of having to share her remaining parent with you. This will seem like another loss on top of the one she has already suffered. However a wise step-parent can teach a child who has been badly hurt to trust again, and this is an invaluable lesson.

The new step-family may encounter all sorts of problems which could be due to what has happened before the step-parent's arrival. The departed parent may have a lot to answer for, but be wary of criticism in front of the child – children are amazingly loyal even to the most abusive and uncaring parents.

As a result of losses and upheaval they have been through as the result of the break-up of the parental relationship, step-children can be difficult and two-faced! A child who was always polite, charming and amusing in the early days of your relationship with the parent may seem to have turned into the child from hell the moment you move in together, and this is something you have to be prepared for. An only child has no brother or sister to confide in and may also have a particularly close relationship with the parent she lives with. It may feel at the beginning very much as though two is company and three is a crowd with both you and the child vying for the parent's attention. On the plus side at least you won't have a whole army of children ganging up on you to make your life a misery!

The relationship between the step-parent and child usually goes through three stages, resentment, suspicion and eventually acceptance. Then, if you're really lucky, love might begin to grow. However these stages do not necessarily follow a linear progression and often you will find it's more a question of one step forward and two steps backward.

The most important thing to remember is not to descend to the child's level. A step-child can become angry and aggressive because he feels insecure. He has already lost one parent and may be terrified of losing either the parent he lives with or the one he has acquired. Therefore it may take what will seem to you an amazing length of time for life to settle down. A child may resort to bad behaviour to get attention and you will need to allow the child to be noticed without need for being troublesome. A good policy is to ignore bad behaviour (unless it is threatening to hurt someone or damage prized possessions) and applaud the good. If you notice how nicely he's been behaving or if he's been particularly helpful, tell him so. Praise and positive encouragement work wonders within fragile relationships.

However, when a child has been naughty it is less damaging to the relationship and the child if punishment or discipline is carried out by the biological parent. The child is used to being told off by her parent and knows that she is nevertheless still loved. She will not have this confidence in a step-parent and may be terrified of having jeopardized the new family relationship especially as she may already have experienced the failure of one family partnership. In spite of what might seem her antipathy towards you, she may, in fact, have high hopes for the new family relationship and yet more reason to fear the worst. On top of which she won't always be in control of her emotions.

If you ever lose your temper or control, always apologize to the child and try to explain your own feelings. Don't rise to the bait when a child throws in the classic line, 'You're not my mum/dad anyway!' A suitable response might be, 'No, I'm not, but I do care very much for you and . . .' Refuse to take rows any more seriously than biological families do and never underestimate the value of an apology.

Obviously a child who is angry and frightened is not showing you her best side, and it may be hard for you to see any redeeming features at times. But remember why you fell in love with her parent; the child is bound to reveal some similar attributes at some stage. Try to understand the child's point of view, encourage her to talk about how she feels and listen to what she has to say. Don't assume you can always supply immediate solutions to her problems – very few biological parents can either – but discuss the issues as far as you can depending on the age of the child. Learning to understand how she feels will lead to increased tolerance. It is important to realize that many feelings and problems are not particular to step-parenting, and many natural parents encounter difficulties.

One way to improve your relationship with the child is to take on some of the tasks the single parent could not do or never got round to. For instance a new father might take a son to a football match, or help a girl with some woodwork. A new mother might offer some expertise she has that the father lacks or hasn't had time for. Time is one of the most important things that a step-parent can make available to a child. Thus you can become gradually and increasingly involved in family life without coming into competition with absent parent. Care can be as important as love. You can't necessarily love a child but you can be thoughtful and give conscientious care. Show commitment, loyalty, friend-ship and companionship and you will be well on the way to having an excellent step-relationship. Begin with liking the child and love will have the opportunity to grow.

THE SEX OF THE STEP-CHILD

As almost all parents bringing up an only child on their own are mothers, the chances are the new step-parent is a male and his role will differ with the age of the child. Sometimes you will find that the child has, in his or her own way, been searching for a father figure anyway so this should make your life easier. However little boys who have lived on their own for some time with their mothers might like to think of themselves as the man of the house and will resent your intrusion. On the other hand you may find you've become the long awaited male influence and the step-son may try to monopolize your time with football and the like. Equally you might find a little girl will overtly flirt with you and sometimes even try to draw your attention away from the mother. However, little girls are just as possessive of their mother's love and might resent any man who comes to share it, terrified that she may lose her parent to you.

STEP-PARENT TRAPS

This is what you must try to avoid in order for your relationship to develop and flourish. Don't:

- deny problems
- attribute everything that goes wrong in relation to the child to being a step or an only
- meet anger with anger
- become aggressive
- project your own thoughts and or fears onto the child
- be too nice (it's not realistic)
- rush (allow enough time to build a relationship with a child)
- take rows any more seriously than biological families do
- forget to allow time for the biological parent and child to be alone together
- ignore existing family or household routines (lack of routine equals havoc and that's the last thing you want to be held responsible for)
- make the child a scapegoat for everything else that may go wrong in your life

- expect too much too soon
- criticize the absent parent
- undermine the biological parent
- be too self-critical
- allow the child to play one adult off against another

FINANCIAL ASPECTS

A step-parent coming into a family should bring an economic improvement. However, this may be the first time the new parent has had to share his or her resources. The parent of the child has been used to making sacrifices, if necessary. This may be an unknown experience for the new partner, who may resent having an income eaten away by family expenditure. You may also find that your new partner may be prone to guilt about the break-up of the earlier relationship and therefore be prone to overindulgence, giving more to the child than is either necessary or required and this is something which will have to be worked on between you (out of the child's hearing) and reduced gradually to a more realistic level.

Money from the absent parent

The absent parent may or may not contribute to the child's upkeep – even with the advent of the Child Support Agency many absent parents still manage to avoid the net. However what frequently happens is that the absent parent sends a large sum of money for birthdays or Christmas (or gives rather grand gifts), as if the gift made up for possibly not seeing the child very often or not taking much of an interest in her life. This can be very hurtful to the parent and step-parent alike and children soon see through this action when they are older.

However younger children may be enthralled, as Ruth pointed out.

> *Harriet never saw that much of her father after we split up and less so after I remarried. When it was her birthday or Christmas he used to phone and ask me what she wanted. I always knew exactly the right thing of course and when she got to open the parcel she always thought her daddy was marvellous and bought her such lovely presents. After a while he stopped seeing her altogether and the presents stopped too. She still talks about him. But one day,*

not long ago, she said to us, 'I don't know why I call him Daddy. He's not a proper daddy. Not like John is.'

Money from grandparents

Grandparents, especially those related to a dead parent, might be prepared to pay for expensive school trips, holidays and fashionable clothes that would otherwise be out of the question. This is fine when there is still only one child in the family but if you and your partner have a baby together you might not wish for them to be treated so differently. This will need sensitive handling. But where feasible contact should be maintained with the relatives of the the ex-partner and compromises should be reached.

CONTACT WITH THE ABSENT BIOLOGICAL PARENT

My mum doesn't talk to my dad at all. It's really between my mum and my step-mum – I can understand them not getting on because my step-mum stops me seeing my mum and all my uncles and aunts. It upsets me because I want my parents to be friends. John, ten

Having two homes is quite nice. Megan, eight

A step-parent inherits an arrangement for contact with the absent parent and this may mean more rearrangements in your life. What you must do is disentangle your own wishes from the needs and desires of the child. Whenever there is any sort of conflict the needs of the child should be paramount, so sometimes it might mean someone having to swallow their pride.

The role of new step-grandparents

Some grandparents are happy to accept step-grandchildren and make no distinction between them and any natural grandchildren they may have. Others may be less accommodating, as Linda found in the case study in the previous chapter. Step-grandparents can be a real help to a child in a new family – they are not so emotionally involved and may be able to explain situations and help out as mediators.

> # Checklist for good step-parenting
> - always consider the age of the child
> - respect privacy – a child may resent your intrusion into her room, always knock, and never walk into a bathroom while she's in there
> - a teenager might appreciate a separate entry in the telephone directory if her name is different from the new family one
> - discuss parenting with your partner and always try to present a united front, a child should understand that you operate as a couple and make joint decisions

GAY COUPLES

Sara and Kate have been together for five years. Kate's daughter, Alicia, is now eight and it was through her that the couple met – Sara was taken on as the nanny just after Kate's relationship with her daughter's father had broken up. Sara talks about her feelings and experiences.

Falling in love with a woman who had a child was a new experience for me but I just rushed in head-first. At the time I didn't really consider the implications or complications. I had been openly gay for about eight years and had decided I never wanted children. I was travelling about a lot – to other countries – and I was always out socializing, seeing films and so on, and suddenly all that had to stop. We couldn't go out as a couple at the drop of a hat and babysitting costs made nights out expensive. Of course I did resent the fact that my life was changing but I always rationalized it: if Kate hadn't had a child I would never have met her.

Alicia and I took some time to settle into our relationship – about two years. I am definitely not another mother in her life. I was quite clear about that. She already has a mother and she didn't need two. I am another significant person in her life. The pitfall for me was that I was being cast, if you like, in the traditional role of the father. I was the one who tended to discipline Alicia. Both of us were guilty of this and also the childminders we had tended to say things like, 'I'll tell Sara when she gets home.' I didn't think this was fair on me or Alicia and I talked to Kate about it. Now I try not to interfere in differences between Alicia and Kate and my relationship with Alicia has improved.

In fact, our relationship gets better as she gets older and we can talk about things on a more conversational level. Sometimes I still resent her presence – I think any couple does – and it does depend on a child's age. However when I do find myself resenting her, I remind myself how selfish I'm being. Kate may be my partner and hopefully a long term one but she's Alicia's mother and you only have one. It makes you feel a bit small.

When Alicia was six or so she resented me. She was very jealous and was convinced Kate loved me more than her. But she seems to have got over that now. What she probably will find hard is getting grief from peers for having a gay parent. That's something we'll have to work through together. I hope it won't be too hard on Alicia – I do love her.

ADOPTING AN ONLY CHILD

In Britain during the 1950s couples were encouraged to adopt two children because it was thought that parents would be over-protective of an only adopted child. Now, because of changes in society, there are fewer babies available for adoption: single women are no longer stigmatized by having a child without a husband and therefore tend to keep their babies while increased reliability in contraception and the legalization of abortion have contributed to a fall in the numbers of babies who are adopted.

Another change in the way adoption is viewed is that agencies now consider single men and women as prospective parents for older children and those with special needs. If you live together as a couple, be it gay or heterosexual, only one partner will be able to legally adopt a child, but both can obviously have a parental role in the child's life.

So does being an only affect how the adopted child feels about her life and family? Apparently not, according to a study published in 1980 by Lois Raynor. A group of 160 adopted children were interviewed as young adults. Of these one third were onlies, one third elder and the rest younger children. Although some of the onlies had wanted siblings the proportion who were satisfied with their adoptive families was the same as for those who did have brothers and sisters. There was no evidence that the adopted only child was any more at risk and that success in terms of family life depended on the parents and how they handled the situation, not the size of the family.

Adopting as a couple

Only if you are married are you allowed to adopt as a couple. If you are in another sort of partnership only one of you will be able to be the adoptive parent. Married couples are more likely to be able to adopt a baby but as mentioned before there are less babies put up for adoption. Also one of the catches of adoption is that a couple will probably be older when they want to adopt as they will have tried for their own family and then gone through fertility tests and many societies have an upper age limit. Also these days the biological mother has more say and may stipulate younger parents as well as continued contact with her offspring. (See the Useful Addresses section at the end of the book for the British Agencies for Adoption and Fostering.)

Adopting as a single parent

Many men and women are now taking advantage of the relaxation in the adoption agency criteria to allow them to adopt. However, unless there are exceptional circumstances a baby would never be offered to a single parent. Many babies offered for adoption are given up by single mothers who feel their baby would have a better life with two parents and stipulate this is what they want for their child.

Babies are sometimes available from other countries and here Caroline recalls her experiences.

> I adopted my son from an orphanage in Mexico at a time when I was living and working in North America. I first met him when he was six months old and the adoption went through when he was nine months. I never had brothers or sisters and had no experience of children so I have little with which to compare bringing up an only child.
>
> When you have one child you have to make sure you feel their need for social contact. Paulo is very self-reliant and has learned to enjoy his own company. And as a single mother it is important to supply strong male role models. However I had to

laugh when Paulo went to a preschool playgroup in Canada. A member of staff said he must have good role models as he had learned to stand at the loo rather than sit down. In fact he had worked this out for himself.

In Canada there was a network of single women who adopted. In fact adoption was encouraged, particularly from Mexico. Our children became a family together.

As an only child myself, while I was living in Canada I was very aware of the importance of family and the extended family although it didn't bother me until I became a mother myself. In Canada friends easily became family but you lack a sense of roots. That was why I came back to this country with Paulo — for the sense of continuity that I didn't have over there. It's healthy to have a sense of family and we also place a strong value on his own roots. We talk about Mexico and what it's like to be Mexican, its culture, food, art and so on.

I think a lot of adoptions of children from other races break down because they don't value the child's heritage. Another problem is having spent his early months in an orphanage Paulo suffered from maternal deprivation and he can be very insecure. Because of this I think he benefits by having a single parent. I can give all my love and attention to him. At eight he's now fine on a one to one basis and with a few children but in a large group like a class room he can be very demanding — he needs to know and is desperate for the teacher to love him the best.

We also have to cope with his feelings of abandonment. But we are overcoming these as we have a very strong home base and he knows I'm always there for him.

My parents adore him but they did have to overcome their racism. Then my father asked me, 'Why didn't you do this years ago?'

SUMMARY

Becoming a parent of an only child means that you're leaping in at the deep end — you haven't had the biological preparation for parenthood. Adopting and step-parenting have distinct as well as similar problems and these need to be worked at sensitively.

Epilogue

IF THERE'S one thing I've discovered as the mother of an only child, it's that everybody else in the world feels they have an automatic right to comment on your family size, offer advice, remark on your parenting skills and even make snide comments. So how do you deal with it? One way is to simply ignore the criticism and smile; another is to get into a debate and put over your point of view.

I always used to react in a rather defensive way, saying things like, 'Of course she isn't lonely or spoilt.' Since I've been researching this book, I've had more ammunition and facts at my fingertips. Now I feel confident enough to say, 'Well, research shows that . . .' Some people are genuinely interested and take on board what you are saying, others will never be convinced that you aren't rearing a spoilt brat. But you can't win them all. What is important is that other people don't unduly influence or upset your child. Even comments like 'I expect it's nice for you to play with your little friend. You must be lonely at home' may sow seeds of doubt in a young child's mind. Hopefully as they grow older, they'll be able to reply that it is nice to be with friends but they are happy with their own company at home as well.

Being or having an only child is not inherently worse or better than being a member of a larger family. What is important, as I have argued throughout this book, is the quality of the parenting and that applies to all family configurations.

Appendix I: Famous only children

Alan Ayckbourn
Clive Barker (writer/artist/filmmaker)
David Blunkett
Betty Boothroyd
Leslie Crowther
Noel Edmonds
Peter Hall
Susan Hill
Adolf Hitler
Anthony Hopkins
John Lennon
Jenni Nimmo (children's author)
Lester Piggott
Tony O'Reilly (Irish entrepreneur)
Michael Ryan (Hungerford killer)
Rebecca Ridgway (first woman to karak round Cape Horn Island)
Chris Tarrant
Barbara Taylor Bradford
Arthur Scargill
John Stapleton
Paula Yates

Appendix II: Bibliography

'Adolescents' perceptions of parental affection: an investigation of only child vs first borns', *Journal of Population: Behaviour, Social & Environmental Issues*, 1978.

A Parents' Guide to the Law, Jeannie Mackie and Lesley Taylor, Penguin, 1990.

Caring for Your Children, M. Herbert, Blackwell, 1985.

The Chosen Child Syndrome, Dr Patricia Lowe, Piatkus Books 1990.

Families and How to Survive Them, Robin Skynner and John Cleese, Methuen, 1983.

Life and How to Survive It, Robin Skynner and John Cleese, Methuen, 1993.

The Lonely, Only Mouse, Wendy Smith, Little Picture Puffin, 1988.

Only Child, Jill Pittkeathley and David Emerson, Souvenir Press, 1994.

The Only Child, Myths and Reality, Ann Laybourn, HMSO, 1994.

The Single Child Family, Toni Fablo (ed.), The Guildford Press, New York, 1984.

Step-parents and Their Children, Stephen Collins, Souvenir Press, 1988.

Children and Society (volume 4, no. 4), 1990.

Master Race, Katrine Clay and Michael Leapman, Hodder and Stoughton, 1995.

Going it Alone, R. S. Weiss, Basic Books, 1979.

The Adopted Child Comes of Age, Lois Raynor, Allen and Unwin, 1980.

Appendix III:
Useful addresses

Loss and bereavement
Compassionate Friends
53 North Street,
Bristol BS3 1EN
0117 9539639

Stillbirth and Neonatal Death Society,
28 Portland Place,
London W1N 4ED
0171 436 5881

Lone Parents
Gingerbread,
35 Wellington Street,
London WC2 7BN
0171 240 0953
(and see local Yellow Pages)

Adoption
British Agencies for Adoption and Fostering
Skyline House,
200 Union Street,
London SE1 0LX

Bullying
KIDSCAPE,
152 Buckingham Palace Road,
London SW1W 9TR
0171 730 3300

General
Exploring Parenthood,
The National Parenting Development Centre,
20a Treadgold Street,
London W11
0171 221 4471
Advice line
0171 221 6681

Index